英语写作教程：以内容为依托
Content-based English Writing
（上册）

邹 涛　张 杨　主编

图书在版编目(CIP)数据

英语写作教程：以内容为依托(上册)/邹涛，张杨主编. —北京：北京大学出版社，2012.11
(21世纪英语专业系列教材)
ISBN 978-7-301-21459-6

Ⅰ.①英…　Ⅱ.①邹…②张…　Ⅲ.①英语－写作－高等学校－教材　Ⅳ.①H315

中国版本图书馆 CIP 数据核字(2012)第 252513 号

书　　　名：英语写作教程：以内容为依托(上册)
著作责任者：邹　涛　张　杨　主编
责 任 编 辑：孙　莹
标 准 书 号：ISBN 978-7-301-21459-6/H・3167
出 版 发 行：北京大学出版社
地　　　址：北京市海淀区成府路 205 号　100871
网　　　址：http://www.pup.cn　电子信箱：zbing@pup.pku.edu.cn
电　　　话：邮购部 62752015　发行部 62750672　编辑部 62754382
　　　　　　出版部 62754962
印 　刷 　者：北京大学印刷厂
经 　销 　者：新华书店
　　　　　　787 毫米×1092 毫米　16 开本　8.25 印张　280 千字
　　　　　　2012 年 11 月第 1 版　2012 年 11 月第 1 次印刷
定　　　价：20.00 元

未经许可，不得以任何方式复制或抄袭本书之部分或全部内容。
版权所有，侵权必究
举报电话：(010)62752024　电子信箱：fd@pup.pku.edu.cn

本教材是"985工程"之"优秀教学团队支持计划"——"英语写作教学团队"(项目编号为 A1098521-029),以及全国教育科学"十二五"规划2011年度教育部重点课题"高校公共英语写作系列课程设计与教学方法研究"(项目编号为 GPA115005)的阶段性成果。

Reading makes a full man; conference a ready man; and writing an exact man.
—Francis Bacon

读书使人充实,讨论使人机敏,写作使人严谨。

——培根

Contents

序言
Introduction to Writing Process and Writing Techniques ········ 1
Chapter One Life Wisdom ········ 1
    Text A The Handsome and Deformed Leg ········ 1
    Text B What I Have Lived for ········ 10
    Text C Half a Sheet of Paper ········ 14
    Corpus-based Exercises (1) ········ 18
Chapter Two Love ········ 21
    Text A Beauty ········ 21
    Text B Going Home ········ 30
    Text C Cyber Love: What Is Real & What Is Virtual ········ 34
    Corpus-based Exercises (2) ········ 38
Chapter Three Family ········ 41
    Text A The Lost Art of Family Traditions ········ 41
    Text B Building a Happy, Healthy Family ········ 50
    Text C Of Parents and Children ········ 54
    Corpus-based Exercises (3) ········ 57
Chapter Four Friendship ········ 62
    Text A Philia ········ 62
    Text B On Friendship ········ 75
    Text C For Immediate Release ········ 82
    Corpus-based Exercises (4) ········ 86
Chapter Five Education ········ 90
    Text A Experience and Education ········ 90
    Text B Why I Teach ········ 102
    Text C Why Chinese Mothers Are Superior ········ 108
    Corpus-based Exercises (5) ········ 113

序　言

在我国，随着哑巴式英语学习的困境逐渐解除，写作环节的问题日益凸显。学生在写作中要么无话可写，要么有话表达不好。那一份份内容空洞、错误频出的英语毕业论文，也许是对写作问题的最好见证。写作老师们变得无所适从，当他们耐心地从词句段篇按步骤分学期讲解时，学生因早早面对各种英语考试中的写作而心急如焚；当部分老师痛下决心扔掉国内教材而与国际接轨时，又发现英文原版教材的很多话题存在明显的水土不服问题。市面上针对考试或特殊用途的写作教材数量繁多，却并不适于基础阶段的写作教学。基于以上困境，本书编委在写作教学改革与实践基础上，试图结合中西写作教材的优势，以编写新教材为牵引带动写作教学模式的革新。

本书编写理念为以内容为依托的教学法（content-based instruction，简称CBI）。不过，这里的"内容"不是某个专门的学科知识，而是适应于基础写作教学需求、让学生感觉亲切而有表达兴趣的话题。CBI教学法在本教材中体现在以下三个方面：

其一，本教材摈弃以写作技巧为纲的传统编写模式，而是通过广泛的问卷调查，选取与学生学习生活密切相关的十大话题为编写框架，以尽可能激起学生讨论和写作的兴趣，让其产生表达的冲动和欲望；

其二，每章精选三篇范文，在文章内容及问题设计上尽可能体现跨文化视野（注意中西文化差异对比）和时代意识（注意传统与当下的对比），兼顾范文的语言质量（语言地道）与思想高度（富有启发性），以便真正激发学生的讨论兴趣并便于写作模仿。

其三，我们在每一章的写作任务设计时紧紧围绕某个具体话题，从词、句、段、章各个层面紧扣该话题进行引导，努力让课文最后的篇章写作任务水到渠成。

其四，为帮助学生掌握每个话题的核心关键词的地道搭配，编委成员自创大学英语语料库，收录目前市面上广泛使用的十余套大学英语教材以及本套教材的选文，通过语料库检索，引导学生对每章话题的关键词进行地道的语言搭配训练。

为解决因以话题为纲而可能带来的技巧训练不成体系这一问题，我们采用了两种策略：

其一，我们在开篇的Introduction部分对写作过程和写作策略进行了整体性的介绍，帮助学生对写作形成一个整体概观。

其二，我们将Introduction中提到的各个层面（词、句、段、章）的写作技巧看作Basic Writing Techniques，以其为线索进行练习设计，将这些技巧在每一章的具体文本中进行阐释、演绎和模仿，使学生在不断的强化中真正领会基本写作技巧的具体应用。所以，请读者不要因每篇出现的技巧分析而厌倦。万变不离其宗，只要你真正学会了从这些角度去思考任何一篇文章，你的阅读和写作能力也水到渠成。

练习设计的具体思路如下：我们强调对学生的批判思维的训练，第一部分Critical reader重在引导学生把握文章主旨并进行思维拓展，努力让学生有话可说、想说。其中的Critical reader A 主要提醒学生阅读过程中需要注意的问题；Critical reader B 主要针对读完全文后的思维拓展。第二部分critical writer重在引导学生理解和掌握思想呈现、表达的方式，让学生有话能说。其中Basic Writing Techniques这部分以Introduction中提到的各个层面的写作技巧为线索，将这些技巧一一运用到每个具体文本中；Specific Writing Techniques这部分针对Basic Writing Techniques练习中未涵盖的其他写作技巧进行阐释和演练。最后以篇章写作任务收尾。

附录一收录了应用文写作范例，为学生的日常英语写作提供帮助；附录二整理出英式英语与美式英语对照简表。负责审校本教材英语部分的美国外教Frederic Cubbage指出，中国学生在口语上学的大都是美式英语，而他们阅读的教材内容却英式美式混杂，导致他们的英语语言输出也是混杂状态，让地道的美国人或英国人感觉很别扭，甚至常常产生误解。他的意见引起我们的反思，意识到中国老师和学生在教与学的过程中确实很容易忽视英式英语与美式英语的差异。有鉴于此，我们制定了附录二，虽然受篇幅所限收录的内容不多，但旨在提醒学生在英语表达过程中注意针对不同的对象而有所选择。

本教材主要供英语专业基础写作课以及非英语专业的优生班英语写作课使用。在进入具体的章节之前，强烈建议读者先认真读完导论，以快速形成一个有关写作的整体认识，这样能很好地理解后面十章和Introduction部分的呼应关系。在话题排序上，我们根据问卷调查结果，按照话题和学生心理距离、熟悉程度程度的降序排列。但是，有些话题之间的差距并不明显，所以，教师或自学者可以根据实际需求选择话题顺序。此外，因为每一章都包括了词、句、段、章各层的写作训练，各章自成一个相对完整的写作训练体系，也加大了使用的灵活性。

本教材编写过程历经两年半。在写作教学改革项目的推动下，我们对编写内容反复思考、讨论、修订和检验，最终形成此稿。不当之处，恳请方家读者指正，以便进一步完善。

本教材编委按章节顺序具体分工如下：邹涛编写导论、第一章，负责全书思路制定和全书审稿；吕汀编写第二章、附录二；袁毅敏编写第三章、参编第九章；王琪欣编写第四章、第五章；肖飞燕编写第六章、附录一；张扬编写第七章，负责提供语料库及使用技术，以及全书格式审校；龙梅编写第八章、主编第九章；邢青编写第十章，参与下册审稿；Frederic Cubbage负责全书英文审校。

邹涛

2012年7月于成都

Introduction to Writing Process and Writing Techniques

I. Writing process[1]

The general writing process may be divided into the following major stages: brainstorming, clustering, thesis formulation, drafting, revising and editing.

1. Brainstorming. When you get a topic to write about, the first thing you may do is to write down every idea that occurs to you, without worrying about the correctness of grammar and spelling. This technique is called brainstorming. For example, Frank's brainstorming on the topic "courting in college life—candy or poison?" resulted in the following list:

Relief homesickness and loneliness

Make life romantic

Time-consuming

Expensive

Encourage each other in difficulties

Heart broken when the relationship fails

Lose chance to make friends with classmates and other people

Play truant

Prove personal magnetism

2. Clustering. After working out a list of ideas like the above one, the next step is to cluster, i.e., to lay out the ideas visually to find connections and to branch out and expand ideas. This step leads to a logical order to organize your ideas. Let's see Frank's clustering:

---

[1] 这部分的很多观点取自陈法春主编,《基础英语写作》,北京大学出版社,2007,第38—44页。

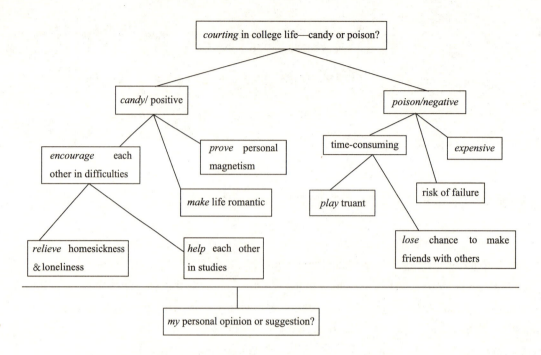

3. Thesis formulation. The thesis statement states the topic of your writing and your opinion on it. It clearly defines the target you are trying to hit, thus keeping you on the subject and avoiding digressions in the process of drafting. After the clustering step, Frank has to consider what direction he wants to choose. He spent some time in figuring out a way out of the dilemma between candy and poison. Then he wrote down his opinion:

Courting in college life has both positive and negative effects. How it will influence you depends on the balance between self-improving and love-searching. To benefit most and risk least from it, make yourself more competitive first, through active participation both in class and in extracurricular activities, then you will win a lover without too much cost both in time and in money, while enjoying the happiness of love.

The first two sentences can be used in the introduction paragraph as a thesis statement, while the third sentence can be used in the conclusion part, echoing and specifying the thesis statement.

4. Drafting. Drafting is to develop the ideas covered in the clustering into a whole, with the guidance of the thesis statement, without concerning about the punctuation, spelling, and grammar. The following tips may help when you draft:

1) Let your draft be rough.
2) Keep focused on the thesis statement when you argue from different perspective.
3) Skip troublesome parts.
4) Return to your clustering step if you can't continue writing, or when new ideas conflicting with the former ones come up.
5) Write as long and as fast as you can.

5. Revising. Revising is a thorough rethinking and reworking of the draft. The following tips may be helpful when you revise:

1) Have I given a clear thesis in the introduction paragraph?

2) Are all my points related to the thesis?

3) Is my argument supported? Do I have specific evidence for each supporting point?

4) Is my essay well organized? Are my points in a logical order and easy for readers to follow?

5) Are there redundant expressions to eliminate?

6) Are there any vague words to substitute by specific ones?

6. Editing. Editing is the process of getting a piece of writing ready for the audience. First, check your writing for grammar, spelling and punctuation. Then, edit your writing according to the required format, including the documentation format (if sources are used), and the printing format.

II. Essential writing techniques[2]

1. Style and word choice

Writing style is basically the author's voice presented through words. It can be affected by the choice of vocabulary, order of words within a sentence, and emphasis through punctuation, all of which help to set the tone. The choices of these elements should reflect the author's purpose, and consider the reader or audience's expectation. The author's purpose may be to explain, to narrate, to persuade, to describe, to illustrate, to define, to analyze, or to entertain. The main purpose of college writings is usually to demonstrate how well a student thinks and understands the given topic.

Four levels of diction. There are four levels of diction:

1) Formal: for highly educated audience; ceremonial, scholarly, or technical purpose.

2) Standard: for educated audience; college papers, business communications, mass publications, and many other writing purposes.

3) Informal: for general audience; spoken rather than written situations, personal letters, conversational and entertaining purposes.

4) Slang: for specific audience; used to enhance the writing through dialogue essential to the character, such as in novels, or to build connections between members of a specific group or generation.

A Standard level is most commonly used, but it does not mean the most formal word should be used, i.e., multi-syllabic, Latin-form, or pretentious. The best approach is to use the standard or common word that conveys the most accurate meaning.

---

2 Many ideas in this part are from Diane M. Coffman ed. *A Peking University Coursebook on English Exposition Writing* （北京大学出版社，2003，第1—83页）.

Pretentious Wording	Common Wording
in regards to	concerning; about
utilize	use
elucidate	explain
prior to	before
because of the fact that	because
ascertain	find out
commence	begin

Eloquent versus practical style. The style can be eloquent or practical. Eloquent style uses more abstract words, a lot of figures of speech, and the arrangement of words in sentences may have more variations than the standard word order. Practical style uses words that are concrete and specific, and the word order is usually standard. For example:

Eloquent style: *After the hungry mountain daffodils drank the mother's milk of newly fallen dew upon the earth's barren soil, they reached their arms upward and turned their yellow faces to the nurturing sun, whilst dancing in the cool breezes from the ocean below.*

Practical style: *After the mountain daffodils absorbed needed moisture from the recent dewfall, they grew quickly in the warm sunlight and swayed in the ocean's cool breezes.*

In the above sentence of practical style, we replace personification used in the eloquent style, with more accurate descriptive phrases and verbs, so the Subject Noun is able to actually do what the Verb means.

Careful use of absolutes. One bad habit is the improper use of absolutes such as *all, only, never, always,* and *nothing*. For example, the sentence "Mary and Rose always go shopping together" implies that Mary and Rose never shop separately, which is probably not true. Then we'd better replace the word always with *frequently*. Therefore, try to use *seldom, usually, occasionally, frequently, often* instead of the absolutes mentioned above.

2. Basic rules for good sentences

1) Unity: one single, complete thought.

Please read the following two sentences and try to find out the problems with them:

(a) *Born in a small town in South China in the early 50s, he grew up to be a famous musician.*

(b) *Yao Ming is one of the greatest basketball players.*

Sentence (a) expresses two thoughts, and more information is needed to connect these two thoughts, while sentence (b) is not a complete thought, since using the comparative or superlative forms of adjectives and adverbs requires the writer to state clearly what items are being compared. They can be revised as the following:

(a') *He was born in a small town in South China in the early 50s. He liked singing very much from childhood and grew up to be a famous musician.*

(b') *Yao Ming is one of the greatest basketball players in the world.*

2) Coherence: clear connection between parts; no faulty parallel constructions, no unknown pronouns, no unclear relationships.

For example, in the sentence "Upon entering the classroom, the students stood up," the relationship is unclear—who entered the classroom? A better sentence would be: When the teacher entered the classroom, the students stood up.

3) Conciseness: no unnecessary words.

Please revise the following two sentences into more concise ones.

(c) *There is an increase of crime in most of the big cities.*

(d) *He returned in the early part of the month of August.*

Many Chinese students like to start a sentence with the "There be…" structure. "There be" are usually redundant words, so it is better to start with the subject. The above two sentences can be revised into:

(c') *Crime is increasing in most big cities.*

(d') *He returned in early August.*

4) Good grammar: good structure, good use of articles (a, an, the), accurate spelling, and clear punctuation.

3. Basic Rules for Good Paragraphs

1) Unity: a central theme; clear topic sentence, and all sentences within the paragraph relate to the topic sentence.

2) Cohesion and Coherence: Cohesion usually means a semantic relation between two elements between and among sentences in a text. Cohesive ties mainly include reference (pronominal, demonstratives, definite article, and comparatives), substitution, ellipsis, conjunction, and lexical reiteration and collocation.[3] For example,

(a) *Mary attracts many classmates' attention, <u>because</u> <u>she</u> is very beautiful.*

conjunction   pronominal

(b) *Don't you like horses? I know you <u>do</u>. Look at <u>that</u> <u>one</u> in your left side.*

ellipsis   demonstrative   substitution

Coherence means each sentence leads smoothly and logically to the next sentence; proper order; no unclear relationships; good transition. Cohesion and coherence interact to a great degree, but a text full of cohesive ties is not necessarily coherent. For example,

(c) *Mary has a dove in her room. Doves are used in many ceremonies. They are very interesting. Her room is beautiful, because of the dove.*

---

3 Stephen P. Witte, Lester Fagley. Coherence, Cohesion, and Writing Quality. *College Composition and Communication,* Vo. 32, No. 2 (1981), *Language Studies and Composing.* pp. 189—204.

3) **Development**: The paragraph has sufficient information to support the topic sentence.

4. Basic rules for good essays
1) A focused introduction section
The elements of an introduction usually include:

Opener: an interesting opening sentence or two that catches the reader's attention, setting up the topic for discussion.

Lead-in: a few sentences that guide the reader from the broad, general topic to the narrow, relevant issue.

Thesis statement: a specific statement of the writer's position on the issue and provides the framework for the essay.

Scope and methods (optional): states what the essay will/will not accomplish or discuss. If the essay is about an experiment or research project, then the methods being used to accomplish the project should also be mentioned.

2) A thorough development section
The development section is where the writer fully develops the content, or thesis. The elements of this section depend on the writing type and the internal structure.

Writing types may include the following:

(a) **Narration**. Narration writing chronicles a series of events. It may be the steps taken in a science experiment, or it may be the adventures happening to the characters in a story. In storytelling, it is possible to break the chronological order of events through flashbacks—memory recall. The purpose of narration may be to prove a theory, illustrate a concept, praise a virtue, condemn a vice, etc.

(b) **Description**. Description writing is to describe, to paint a picture in words of a person, object, place, or scene. It is developed through sensory details, or the impressions of one's senses: seeing, hearing, tasting, feeling, and smelling. Scientific description may describe the item's qualities (sour, sweet, blue, red, loud or soft in decibels, hard or soft in compression). Evocative description recreates the feelings.

(c) **Illustration**. Illustration writing is the most common writing type. It is used every time an example is given. Good examples help to clarify a writer's thought by making the general specific, and the abstract concrete. Examples should be wisely selected, sufficient, specific, and typical, and there must be a logical sequence if multiple examples are given.

(d) **Definition**. Definition writing clarifies abstract terms or concepts by presenting the essential nature and qualities of the concept, or by showing how the concept is different from others like it.

(e) **Persuasion/Argumentation**. Persuasion/Argumentation writing is used to convince the reader of the writer's point of view or assertion, to persuade the reader to change his mind or behavior, to approve a policy, or to take a course of action. It uses evidence and facts, forceful language, reasoning and logic to influence others. To reach this purpose, the most compelling points, the most familiar or easily understood points are usually presented first, and the least compelling point, the least familiar or most difficult to understand last.

For each writing type, especially for Persuasion/Argumentation writing, good logic is very important. All the facts and reasons given as evidence should be logically connected with each other and with the conclusion. Any fallacy in logic or wrong step in reasoning would leave the reader in doubt about the whole argument. Generally, there are two types of reasoning: inductive reasoning and deductive reasoning. Inductive reasoning moves from specific facts to a more general conclusion, while deductive reasoning moves from a general statement to a specific conclusion.

After deciding the writing type, the writer should select the structure that best suits the purpose of the essay:

(i) **Compare and Contrast**: to develop your idea by looking at the difference between two or more similar subjects or aspects. When using this structure, keep in mind that only items of the same general class should be compared, and each item should be given balanced treatment.

(ii) **Cause and Effect**: to develop your idea by analyzing what is the cause and what effect has or will follow as result. Cause writing begins with an introduction which briefly describes the effect(s), and then details the cause(s), while Effect writing reverses the structure. Keep in mind that most effects have complicated causes, so do not over-simplify causes and avoid using absolutes. It is not necessary to explore all the direct and indirect causes and effects, so try to give more space to major ones and stop at a place where your purpose has been fulfilled.

(iii) **Division and Classification**: to develop your idea by looking at the organization of the subject; breaking the subject down and dealing with the pieces, or grouping by classification. Division is used to deal with one thing by separating it into parts, while classification is to organize things systematically that share certain qualities. Keep in mind that apply the division/classification consistently and thoroughly, and avoid overlapping.

Then, select **the logical order** in which to present the information:

(i) **Point by Point**. Discuss each item/subject under each of the points the writer is making. This order is preferable in long essays where many aspects are discussed.

(ii) **Subject by Subject**. Discuss all of the various aspects of one subject before moving on to the next item/subject. This order works best in short essays where few aspects are considered, or where the writer's interest is in the whole, rather than in detailed parts.

3) A summarizing conclusion section

The elements of a conclusion usually include:

Summarizing the main points. Reference is made to different parts of the essay and the relationship between one part and another. Keep in mind that new information should not be introduced in this part. Any new information that comes out while drafting this part should be moved to the Development section.

Restating the author's position/opinion (Thesis Statement) and purpose of the essay, verifying that the purpose has been fulfilled.

Looking into the future for possible developments and suggesting a course of action.

Since an article may consist of just one paragraph, and a paragraph one sentence, the basic rules for good sentences, paragraphs and articles can be overlapped and interwoven.

5. Use Critical Thinking in Reading and Writing

Critical thinking has been described popularly as "thinking about thinking". It is about the willingness and ability in questioning. It is the art of analyzing and evaluating thinking with a view to improving it. It does not mean criticizing negatively, but means evaluating your own and others' thinking with an open mind and by applying "intellectual standards of reasoning".

Following are questions that provide intellectual standards of reasoning:

1) All reasoning has a **purpose**. Relevant questions can be: *What is your/ my/their purpose in doing…? What is the objective of this…?*

2) All reasoning is an attempt to settle some **question**, to solve some problem. Relevant questions can be: *What is the question I am/ the author is trying to answer? Is the question clear? Is it complex?*

3) All reasoning is based on some **basic assumptions**. Recognize that all questions and thinking presupposes prior questions and thinking. Then seek to understand the foundation for what is said or believed through answering *"On what do you base your belief?" "What assumption is leading me to this conclusion?" "To answer this complex question, what other questions need to be answered first?"*

4) All reasoning is done from some **point of view**. One of the hallmarks of the critical thinker is a willingness to enter into any and every viewpoint, and then to change one's views when evidence warrants a change. Relevant questions can be: *Is there any other way to look at this situation? How do others view this? What does my/the author's point of view ignore? Am I uncritically assuming that the point of view of the person/author/ instructor/society is justified?*

5) All reasoning is done in a **network** of connected thoughts. For example, *"If what you say is true, wouldn't x or y also be true?"*

6) **Presentation** of thoughts is crucial for the influence of one's ideas upon others. Treat all presentation as in need of development. Relevant questions can be: *Could this be elaborated on or restated for better understanding? Are the concepts used carefully and precisely? Can the readers/audience be attracted at the very beginning? Are the arguments in a logical order easy for others to follow? Is the conclusion satisfactory to the readers/audience?*

Chapter One

Life Wisdom

Warming up

1. Happiness is always what we long for. Describe to your group the happiest and/or the most miserable moments in your life. According to such moments, try to figure out your definition of happiness.
2. Many people like to choose a motto and live under the influence of it in pursuing happiness. What kind of mottoes have you ever chosen, or would like to choose, for your life?
3. If you met a person with one handsome leg and the other deformed, what would be your spontaneous reaction? Would you pay more attention to the deformed leg and ask him or her about it?

Text A

The Handsome and Deformed Leg

By Benjamin Franklin

A Critical Reader (I)

1. There are two types of people in the world. Although they have equal degrees of health and wealth and the other comforts of life, <u>one becomes happy, and the other becomes miserable</u>. This arises from the different ways in which they consider things, persons, events, and the resulting effects upon their minds.

2. In whatever situation men can be placed, they may find conveniences and inconveniences. In whatever company, they may find persons and conversations more or less pleasing. At whatever table, they may find meat and drink of better and worse taste, dishes better or worse prepared. In whatever climate, they may find good and bad weather. Under whatever government, they may find good or bad laws, and good and bad administration of these laws. In whatever poem or work of genius, they may see beauties and faults. In almost every face and every person, they may discover fine features and defects, good and bad qualities.

1. Do you know of any persons who would fit into Franklin's two categories? Can you remember any details about him/her to illustrate such a feature?

2. Can you provide more supporting details, besides those listed in Paragraph 2?

3. Under these circumstances, the people who are to be happy fix their attention on the conveniences of things, the pleasant parts of conversation, the well-prepared dishes, the goodness of the wines, the fine weather. They enjoy all the cheerful things. Those who are to be unhappy think and speak only of the contrary things. Therefore, they are continually discontented themselves. By their remarks, they sour the pleasures of society, offend many people, and make themselves disagreeable everywhere. If this turn of mind were founded in nature, such unhappy persons would be the more to be pitied. <u>The disposition[1] to criticize and be disgusted is perhaps taken up originally by imitation.</u> It grows into a habit, unknown to its possessors. The habit may be strong, but it may be cured when those who have it are convinced of its bad effects on their congeniality[2]. I hope this little admonition[3] may be of service to them, and help them change this habit. Although in fact it is chiefly an act of the imagination, it has serious consequences in life, since it brings on real grief and misfortune. These people offend many others, nobody loves them, and no one treats them with more than the most common civility and respect, and scarcely that. This frequently puts them in bad humor and draws them into disputes. If they aim at obtaining some advantage in rank or fortune, nobody wishes them success. Nor will anyone stir a step or speak a word to favor their ambitions. If they incur[4] public censure[5] or disgrace, no one will defend or excuse them, and many will join to aggravate[6] their misconduct. These people should change this bad habit and condescend[7] to be pleased with what is pleasing, without fretting[8] themselves and others. If they do not, it will be good for others to avoid an acquaintance with them. Otherwise, it can be disagreeable and sometimes very inconvenient, especially when one becomes entangled in their quarrels.

4. An old philosopher friend of mine grew very cautious from experience, and carefully avoided any contact with such people. He had a thermometer[9] to show him the temperature, and a barometer[10] to show when the weather was likely to be good or bad. Since there is no instrument, however, to discover an unpleasant disposition in a person at first sight, he made use of his legs. One of his legs was remarkably handsome, the other, by some accident, was crooked and deformed. If a stranger looked at his ugly leg more than his handsome one, he doubted him. <u>If he spoke

3 Do you agree with the author's statement underlined in Paragraph 3? Do you have more to say?

4 What do you think of the narrator's friend's judgment underlined in Paragraph 4? Please examine your spontaneous reaction in this kind of situation.

of it and took no notice of the handsome leg, my friend had sufficient reason not to bother with him any longer.

5. Not everyone has this two-legged instrument, but everyone, with a little attention, may observe signs of that kind of fault-finding disposition and make the same resolution to avoid those infected with it. I therefore advise those critical, argumentative, discontented, unhappy people, that if they wish to be respected and loved by others, and happy in themselves, they should stop looking at the ugly leg.

Notes

1. disposition /ˌdɪspəˈzɪʃən/ n.   a general tendency of character, behaviour, etc.
2. congeniality /kənˌdʒiːniˈæləti/ n.   agreeable nature, disposition or tastes.
3. admonition /ˌædməˈnɪʃən/ n.   (formal) gentle scolding or warning.
4. incur /ɪnˈkɜː/ v.   to experience something unpleasant as a result of something you have done.
5. censure: (formal) severe criticism of someone.
6. aggravate /ˈæɡrəveɪt/   to make worse, especially a situation or a medical condition.
7. condescend /ˌkɔndɪˈsɛnd/ v.   (often disapproving) to do sth that you think it is below your social or professional position to do.
8. fret: worry about something continuously.
9. thermometer /θəˈmɔmɪtə:/ n.   an instrument used for measuring the temperature of the air, a person's body, etc.
10. barometer /bəˈrɔmɪtə:/ n.   an instrument for measuring air pressure to show when the weather will change.

A Critical Reader (II)

1 If you have a friend or a family member who is somewhat cynical and fault-finding, does he/she suffer all the consequences Franklin has mentioned in the above essay? Is it possible that such kind of habit may also lead to beneficial results if used in other ways? What's your advice then?

2 Think about the most miserable moments mentioned in group discussion in the warming up section again. Is it possible to regard them as a kind of blessing? How might the persons in question benefit from the miserable experiences?

A Critical Writer

I. Basic Writing Techniques

1. Style and word choice

1.1 The above essay is written for _____ (A. common B. highly educated C. local) people. The purpose of the author is to _____ (A. narrate B. persuade C. describe D. entertain) _____

_____. Therefore, the general style of this essay is ____ (A. casual B. standard C. formal). Such a style is reflected in the choice of vocabulary and order of words within a sentence. There is a high percentage of_____(A. Latin B. French C. Anglo-Saxon) _____ (A. monosyllabic or bi-syllabic B. multi-syllabic) words, which English-speaking people have known since childhood, and are close to their hearts and emotionally charged. The structure of most sentences follows the standard word order of:

Subject → Predicate;
Adjective → Object;
Adverb → Verb.

1.2 Look at the following sentence: *He had a thermometer to show him the temperature, and a barometer to show when the weather was likely to be good or bad.* The percentage of multi-syllabic vocabulary is comparatively higher than the other parts in the sentence, due to the two scientific words *thermometer* and *barometer*. Generally speaking, multi-syllabic English words of Latin, Greek or French origin are words of science, religion and official communication. They often help to create the effect of coolness, dignity, formality and intellectual distance.[1] In this essay, the above sentence imbues the narrator's friend with a scientific objectiveness.

2. Basic rules for good sentences and paragraphs

2.1 Conciseness: no redundant words.

Please read Paragraph 1 again. Can you find any redundant words in each sentence of Paragraph 1?

2.2 Unity in a paragraph:

A central theme; clear topic sentence, and all sentences within the paragraph relate to the topic sentence.

What's the topic sentence of Paragraph 1? How the other sentences relate to the topic sentence?

2.3 Cohesion and Coherence:

Cohesion means semantic relationship established through reference (pronominal, demonstratives, definite article, and comparatives), substitution, ellipsis, conjunction, and lexical

---

[1] 参见董启明,《新编英语文体学教程》,北京:外语教学与研究出版社,2008,第28页。

reiteration and collocation. Coherence means each sentence leads smoothly and logically to the next sentence.

In Paragraph 1, how are cohesion and coherence achieved?

2.4 Analysis:

Paragraph 1 is a good example of conciseness, unity, cohesion and coherence.

Sentence 1 (topic sentence): *There are two types of people in the world.*

↓
[The controlling idea]

Sentence 2 (more specific explanation of the topic sentence): *Although they have equal degree of health*

[Cohesion: conjunction]   [Cohesion: pronominal]

and wealth and the other comforts of life, one becomes happy, the other becomes miserable.

[Cohesion: substitution of "some of them"]   [Cohesion: substitution; collocation]

Sentence 3 (causes to the phenomenon mentioned in Sentence 2): *This arises from the different ways in*

[Cohesion: pronominal]   [Cohesion: lexical reiteration of "two" in Sentence 1]

which they consider things, persons, and events, and the resulting effects upon their minds.

2.5 Exercises:

1) To get a better understanding of the writing techniques and resulting effect, please compare the following paragraph with Paragraph 1, and explain the differences between them. Then, revise it in your words, and compare your version with Paragraph 1.

There are happy people and there are miserable people in the world. Things, persons, and events can be considered in different ways. They have the same degree of health, the same degree of wealth, and the same comforts of other kinds, but they consider them positively or negatively. This has different effects upon them.

Your revision:

_____

_____

_____

2) **Imitation:** Please translate the following Chinese into English, imitating the writing techniques in Paragraph 1.

1) 我们学校有两种学生最引人注目。他们智力水平和学习能力不相上下，但一种成为老师的宠儿，一种却让老师感到头疼。这源自于他们发挥其聪明才智的不同方向以及由此给他们自己及其他同学带来的不同影响。

_____

2) 学生最爱议论的有两种老师。他们一样地关心爱护学生，但一种让学生爱上学习，另一种却让学生进一步厌学。这源自于……（请用英文补充完整）

3. Basic rules for good essays: Well-organized structure

3.1 Questions:

1) The information about "the handsome and deformed leg" has not been mentioned until the last two paragraphs. Why does the author choose the title "The Handsome and Deformed Leg"? What are the advantages and disadvantages (if there are) of this title? Can you provide any other alternatives?

2) Benjamin Franklin tries to persuade his readers to get rid of or avoid the frustrating fault-finding habit. How does the author reach this purpose? Can you find out the thesis statement and draw a clustering map to figure out the logical flow of this essay?

3.2 Analysis: The logical flow (unity and coherence):

This essay is well-organized, with a focused Introduction (Paragraph 1), an effective Development section (Paragraph 2—4) and a summarizing Conclusion (Paragraph 5)

Paragraph 1: A focused introduction. The first sentence, "There are two types of people in the world," functions as an Opener, setting up the topic for discussion and attracting the readers at once. The second sentence, "Although they have equal degree of health and wealth and the other comforts of life, one becomes happy, the other becomes miserable," is a Lead-in, specifying the "two types". The third sentence, "This arises from the different ways in which they consider things, persons, and events, and the resulting effects upon their minds," serves as the overarching thesis statement, implying that the following parts will discuss "the different ways" first and "the resulting effects" next.

Paragraph 2: Illustrates the potential binary opposites of "things, persons, and events".

Paragraph 3: The author first contrasts the two types of people's different choices between the binary opposites listed in Paragraph 2, and the resulting effects (Sentence 1—5). Then, he discusses the possible causes of the unhappy habit (Sentence 6—8), and argues that exposure to the consequences of such bad habit is a good way to help the possessors to get rid of it (Sentence 9). Thus comes the author's motivation to write this essay (Sentence 10). Correspondingly, in the following part of this paragraph, the author emphasizes the corrosive effects of that bad habit.

Paragraph 4: Provides a specific example to illustrate the consequence of the fault-finding habit. Since the example shows a common phenomenon in daily life and provides a mirror for readers to check their own subconscious behavior, the admonition conveyed by it is very impressive to the readers, helping to fulfill the author's purpose of persuasion (Paragraph 5).

Paragraph 5: The Conclusion section. Sentence 1 summarizes the main points from the specific to the general, while sentence 2 restates the author's opinion, echoing and further clarifying the thesis statement.

Good transition between paragraphs helps to achieve unity and coherence:

This arises from <u>the different ways in which they consider things, persons, and events, and the resulting effects upon their minds.</u> (The last sentence in Paragraph 1)

<u>Under these circumstances</u>, the people who are to be happy fix their attention on the conveniences of things, the pleasant parts of conversation, the well-prepared dishes, the goodness of the wines, the fine weather. (The first sentence of Paragraph 3)

An old philosopher friend of mine grew very cautious from experience, and carefully avoided any contact <u>with such people</u>. (The first sentence of Paragraph 4)

Not everyone has <u>this two-legged instrument</u>, but everyone, with a little attention, may observe signs of that kind of fault-finding disposition and make the same resolution to avoid those infected with it. (The first sentence of Paragraph 5)

3.3 Working out an outline:

Please work out an outline on the topic "Two Types of Students" according to the analysis above. You may resort to the "Writing Process" in the Introduction of this book. Your writing plan should address at least the following questions:

1) How many parts and paragraphs do you plan to write?

2) What is the main idea for each paragraph?

3) What kind of details will you use to illustrate the typical features of these two types of students?

II. Specific Writing Techniques

1. Persuading by comparison and contrast

The author writes an essay to reach one or more purposes: to inform, persuade, entertain, explain, or merely express an idea, feeling, or impression. Persuasion writing is used to convince the reader of the writer's point of view, to persuade the reader to accept the author's suggestions: to change his mind or behavior, to approve a policy, to take a course of action, etc.

Persuasion requires forceful language, reasoning and logic. One effective way to do this is to organize your argumentation by comparison and contrast, especially by contrast. To compare is to examine the similarities between two subjects while to contrast is to find out the differences that set them apart. If you want to persuade the reader to do A, you'd better tell them what kind of consequences if they do B or C rather than A, and you need sufficient evidence to show the differences between them. What's more, all the supporting details given as evidence should be logically connected with each other and with the conclusion.

Contrast forms the basic internal structure of the above essay. Please examine the essay in more depth and try to understand the convincing force produced by contrast.

Please read Paragraph 2 again and pay attention to the power of contrast and parallel.

In whatever situation men can be placed, they may find conveniences and inconveniences. In whatever company, they may find persons and conversations more or less pleasing. At whatever table, they may find meat and drink of better and worse taste, dishes better or worse prepared. In whatever climate, they may find good and bad weather. Under whatever government, they may find good or bad laws, and good and bad administration of these laws. In every poem or work of genius, they may see beauties and faults. In almost every face and every person, they may discover fine features and defects, good and bad qualities.

2. Imitation:

Please translate the following paragraph into English, imitating the writing techniques in Paragraph 2.

不管是读几年级，一种学生自律而另一种学生放任自我。不管是学习什么科目，一种学生觉得有用而另一种学生觉得是浪费时间。不管是……，一种学生……另一种学生……（请用英文补充完整）

_____
_____
_____
_____

3. Read Paragraph 3 again and rewrite it according to the context.

Under these circumstances, the people who are to be happy fix their attention on the conveniences of things, the pleasant parts of conversation, the well-prepared dishes, the goodness of the wines, the fine weather. They enjoy all the cheerful things. Those who are to be unhappy think and speak only of the contrary things. Therefore, they are continually discontented themselves. By their remarks, they sour the pleasures of society, offend many people, and make themselves disagreeable everywhere. If this turn of mind were founded in nature, such unhappy persons would be the more to be pitied. The disposition to criticize and be disgusted is perhaps taken up originally by imitation. It grows into a habit, unknown to its possessors. The habit may be strong, but it may be cured when those who have it are convinced of its bad effects on their congeniality. I hope this little admonition may be of service to them, and help them change this habit. Although in fact it is chiefly an act of the imagination, it has serious consequences in life, since it brings on real grief and misfortune. These people offend many others, nobody loves them, and no one treats them with more than the most common civility and respect, and scarcely that. This frequently puts them in bad humor and draws them into disputes. If they aim at obtaining some advantage in rank or fortune, nobody wishes them success. Nor will anyone stir a step or speak a word to favor their ambitions. If they incur public censure or disgrace, no one will defend or excuse them, and many will join to aggravate their misconduct. These people should change this bad habit and condescend to be pleased with what is pleasing, without fretting themselves and others. If they do not, it will be good for others to avoid an acquaintance with them. Otherwise, it can be disagreeable and sometimes very inconvenient, especially when one becomes entangled in their quarrels.

Rewrite: In Paragraph 3, the author attempts to persuade the readers to form a habit of looking at the bright side of the world by highlighting the consequences of the contrary habit. Please rewrite this paragraph by highlighting the advantages of the good habit, furthering your understanding of the power of contrast in persuasion.

Under these circumstances, the people who are to be **unhappy** fix their attention on _____
_____
_____. They _____. Those who are to be **happy** think and speak only of the contrary things. Therefore, they are continually ___
_____. By their remarks, they _____ the pleasures of society, _____. If this turn of mind were founded in nature, such happy persons would _____. The disposition to **praise and be pleased may be difficult to form**, but it may be taken up by imitation when those who do not have it are convinced of _____. Although in fact it is chiefly an act of the imagination, it has _____ in life, since it brings on real _____. These people _____ many others, nobody _____ them, and no one treats them with _____. This frequently puts them in _____. If they aim at obtaining some advantage in rank or fortune, _____. If they **are confronted with crisis,** _____
_____. **People who tend to be pessimistic should try their best to form this good habit** and learn to be pleased with what is pleasing, without fretting themselves and others. If they **succeed**, it can be _____, especially when one becomes entangled in **difficulties**.

III. Your Turn to Write

Please write an essay on the topic about two typical kinds of students or teachers or parents in three paragraphs: Imitate Paragraph 1 of Franklin's text for your introduction part; describe the contrastive behaviors and manners of these two kinds of people in the second paragraph; discuss the corresponding results and effects of such behaviors and manners upon the relative persons, and provide your suggestion in the last paragraph.

Pearls of Wisdom

1. To be upset over what you don't have is to waste what you do have. —Ken S. Keyes Jr.

2. Life consists not in holding good cards, but in playing well those you hold. —Josh Billings

3. Of all the things you wear, your expression is the most important. —Janet Lane

Text B

Warming up

1. What have you lived for? Think about this question for several minutes before you read the text.
2. Virtues, merits and writing（立德，立功，立言）are the three most important goals many Chinese people have ever lived for. Which historical personages, do you think, have achieved these three goals? And why?
3. The following text is the Prologue to *The Autobiography of Bertrand Russell* (1967). Though mainly identified as a philosopher, logician, mathematician, historian, and social critic rather than a writer of literary works, Russell was awarded the Nobel Prize in Literature in 1950, in recognition of his beautiful and significant writings in which he champions humanitarian ideals and freedom of thought. Can you feel his combined ingeniousness in intelligence and linguistic art from the following text?

What I Have Lived for

By Bertrand Russell

A Critical Reader (I)

1. Three passions, simple but overwhelmingly strong, have governed my life: the longing for love, the search for knowledge, and unbearable pity for the suffering of mankind. These passions, like great winds, have blown me hither and thither[1], in a wayward course, over a great ocean of anguish[2], reaching to the very verge of despair.

2. I have sought love, first, because it brings

ecstasy—ecstasy so great that I would often have sacrificed all the rest of life for a few hours of this joy. I have sought it, next, because it relieves loneliness—that terrible loneliness in which one shivering[3] consciousness looks over the rim[4] of the world into the cold unfathomable[5] lifeless abyss[6]. I have sought it finally, because in the union of love I have seen, in a mystic miniature[7], the prefiguring[8] vision of the heaven that saints and poets have imagined. This is what I sought, and though it might seem too good for human life, this is what—at last—I have found.

3. With equal passion I have sought knowledge. I have wished to understand the hearts of men. I have wished to know why the stars shine. And I have tried to apprehend the Pythagorean[9] power by which number holds sway[10] above the flux.[11] A little of this, but not much, I have achieved.

4. Love and knowledge, so far as they were possible, led upward toward the heavens. But always pity brought me back to earth. Echoes of cries of pain reverberate[12] in my heart. Children in famine, victims tortured by oppressors, helpless old people a burden to their sons, and the whole world of loneliness, poverty, and pain make a mockery of what human life should be. I long to alleviate[13] this evil, but I cannot, and I too suffer.

5. This has been my life. I have found it worth living, and would gladly live it again if the chance were offered me.

1 What's the significance of love to you? Do you have other reasons different from Russell's for pursuing love?

2 In Paragraph 3, the author specifies his purpose for seeking knowledge. Can you give more examples?

Notes

1. **hither and thither** /ˈhɪðə ənd ˈðɪðə/ *adv.* (literary) in many different directions.
   wayward: (written) difficult to control; unpredictable
2. **anguish**: (formal) feeling of great physical or emotional pain
3. **shiver** /ˈʃɪvə/ *v.* (with sth.) to shake slightly because you are cold, frightened, excited, etc.
4. **rim**: edge.
5. **unfathomable** /ʌnˈfæðəməbl/ *a.* (formal) immeasurable; impossible to understand
6. **abyss** /əˈbɪs/ *n.* a large deep hole that appears to have no bottom
7. **miniature** /ˈmɪnətʃə/ *n.* a very small model of something that is usually much larger
8. **Prefigure**: (formal) to suggest or show sth that will happen in the future
9. **Pythagorean** /paɪˌθæɡəˈriːən/ *adj.* of, or associated with the Greek philosopher Pythagoras
10. **hold sway**: to have a dominant influence. **flux**: continuous movement and change
11. **flux** /flʌks/ *n.* (a state of) changing or flowing

12. **reverberate** /[rɪ'və:bə,reɪt/ *v.* (of a sound) to be repeated several times as it bounces off different surfaces.
13. **alleviate** /ə'liːvi,eɪt/ *v.* (written) to make sth. less painful, severe, or serious.

A Critical Reader (II)

1. It is natural that love and knowledge make life meaningful. Does understanding pity for others' misfortunes without the capability to relieve them still make life worth living?
2. Which one of Russell's categories of passions impressed you most? Use evidence from the essay to explain your answer.
3. Wang Yangming（王阳明）is regarded by many Chinese people as one who achieved the three goals of virtues, merits and writing. Can you compare Bertrand Russell with him? What are the similarities and differences between them?

A Critical Writer

I. Style and Word Choice

1. In accordance with the major topic—passion, a lot of powerful words are used to convey strong feelings. Take Paragraph 1 as an example:

Three passions, simple but <u>overwhelmingly strong</u>, have governed my life: the longing for love, the search for knowledge, and <u>unbearable pity</u> for the suffering of mankind. These passions, like <u>great winds</u>, have blown me hither and thither, in a wayward course, over <u>a great ocean of anguish</u>, reaching to <u>the very verge of despair</u>.

2. Please find from the text at least three other expressions of strong feelings and pay attention to the collocation.

Example: loneliness, terrible loneliness, relieve loneliness.

_____
_____
_____
_____

3. Figures of speech

Model: These passions, like great winds, have blown me hither and thither, in a wayward course, over a great ocean of anguish, reaching to the very verge of despair.

Imitation: I fell in love with her. This passion, like big waves, _____ _____. Whenever I saw her, I was like an ant floating in a boundless ocean of honey, overwhelmed with a mixed feeling of _____ _____, struggling to _____ _____.

II. Good Structure in the Level of Paragraph and Essay

1. This essay is well-organized, with a focused Introduction (Paragraph _____), an effective Development section (Paragraph _____) and a summarizing Conclusion (Paragraph _____)

Please explain how each paragraph leads smoothly and logically to the next one.

2. Paragraph 2 explains the reasons why love is well worth living for, by specifying the benefits love can bring. Please rewrite it by emphasizing the consequences of the lack of love. In your rewriting, try to make best use of the original text both in diction and structure:

The original version:

I have sought love, first, because it brings ecstasy—ecstasy so great that I would often have sacrificed all the rest of life for a few hours of this joy. I have sought it, next, because it relieves loneliness—that terrible loneliness in which one shivering consciousness looks over the rim of the world into the cold unfathomable lifeless abyss. I have sought it finally, because in the union of love I have seen, in a mystic miniature, the prefiguring vision of the heaven that saints and poets have imagined. This is what I sought, and though it might seem too good for human life, this is what—at last—I have found.

Rewriting:

Love is what I have sought. Without love, you will not enjoy ecstasy—ecstasy so great that you may be willing to sacrifice all the rest of your life for a few hours of this joy. Without love, _____

Without love, _____

Therefore, _____.

3. Paragraph 3 shows a standard structure: the first sentence is the topic sentence and the following three sentences list three kinds of specific knowledge to be sought. Please add at least two new items of knowledge you wish to obtain.

With equal passion I have sought knowledge. I have wished to understand the hearts of men. I have wished to know why the stars shine. And I have tried to apprehend the Pythagorean power by which number holds sway above the flux. I am eager to _____.

And I have a burning desire for _____.

III. Your Turn to Write

What kind of passion has ever governed your life? Have you experienced different passions in different life phases? Which passion would you like to hold onto through your life? Please write your own version by imitating the writing techniques of Russell's essay.

Pearls of Wisdom

1. Zeal without knowledge is a runaway horse. —Anonymous
2. What makes life dreary is the want of motive. —George Eliot
3. Nothing in life is to be feared. It is only to be understood. —Marie Curie

Text C

Half a Sheet of Paper

By Johan August Strindberg

A Critical Reader

1. The last moving van[1] had gone; the tenant[2], a young man with mourning band around his hat, wandered through the empty rooms to see if anything had been left behind. No, nothing had been forgotten, nothing. He went out into the corridor, determined never to think again of all he had passed through in this apartment. But there, on the wall, near the telephone, was a slip of paper covered with writing. The entries were in several handwriting; some quite legible[3], in black ink; some pencil scrawls[4] in black and red and blue. There stood recorded the whole beautiful romance that had been lived in the short space of two years. All that he had resolved to forget was written there—a bit of human history on half a sheet of paper.

2. He took the sheet down. It was a piece of sun-yellow scratch paper that casts a sheen[5]. He laid it on the mantel[6] of the fireplace in the living room, and bending over, he began to read.

3. First stood her name: *Alice*—the most beautiful name he knew, because it was the name of his

[1] What kind of mood is this young man in?

sweetheart. Beside it was a number, *1511*—it looked like a chant[7] number on the hymn board in church.

4. Underneath was scribbled: The Bank. It was there his work lay, the sacred work which for him meant bread, home, family—the foundations of life. A heavy black line had been drawn across the number, for the bank had failed, and he had been taken on at another, after a short period of much anxiety.

5. Then followed *the livery stable*[8] *and the florist*—That was when they were engaged, and he had a pocketful money.

6. *The furniture dealer—The decorator*—They furnish their apartment. *Express Bureau*—They move in. *Opera House Box Office, 5050.*—They are newly married and go to the opera on Sunday evenings. Their most delightful hours are those spent there, sitting quietly, while their hearts commune in the beauty and harmony of the fairyland on the other side of the footlights.

7. Here followed the name of a man (crossed out), a friend who had risen high, but who fell—dazzled by prosperity—fell irremediably, and had to flee the country. So ephemeral[9] is that will-o'-the-wisp[10], success!

8. Now something new came into the lives of the couple. Entered with a pencil in a woman's hand stands *The Sister.* What sister? Ah! The one with long gray cloak and the sweet, sympathetic face, who comes so softly and never goes through the drawing room, but takes the corridor way to the bedroom. Below her name is written: *Dr. L—*

9. Here first appeared on the list a relative—*Mother.* That is his mother-in-law, who had discreetly[11] kept away so as not to disturb the newly married. But now she has been called, and comes gladly, since she is needed.

10. Then came some entries in red and blue pencil. *Employment Agency.* The maid has left, and a new one must be engaged. *The Apothecary*[12]—H-m! It begins to look dark. *The diary*—Milk is ordered, sterilized milk. *The grocer, the butcher*, and others. The household affairs are being conducted by telephone. Then the mistress of the house is not at her usual post? No. She is confined to her bed.

11. That which followed he could not read, for it grew dim before his eyes, as it must for the drowning man at sea who would look through salt water. But there it stood

2 What's the function of Paragraph 7 in the whole plot?

recorded, in plain, black letters: *The undertaker*[13].

12. That tells enough! —a large and a smaller casket. And in parenthesis was written: "*Of dust.*"

13. There was nothing more. It ended in dust, the way of all flesh.

14. <u>He took up the sun-yellow paper, kissed it, folded it carefully, and put it in his breast pocket.</u>

15. In two minutes he had relived two years of his life.

16. But he was not bowed down as he walked out. On the contrary, <u>he carried his head high, like a proud and happy man,</u> for he knew that to him it had been given to hold for a little the best that life can bestow on man. How many there were, alas! Who had not had this.

3 What change in the man's mood is implied by the series of action described in Paragraph 14?

4 Do you think the man's change is plausible?

Notes

1. **van** /væn/ *n.* a vehicle used for carrying goods or several people. It is usually larger than a car and smaller than a truck, and the back part is enclosed.
2. **tenant** /ˈtɛnənt/ *n.* someone who rents an apartment, house, office, piece of land, etc. from the person who owns it.
3. **legible** /ˈlɛdʒəbəl/ *adj.* able to be read.
4. **scrawl** /skrɔːl/ *v.* to scribble; to write something carelessly or in a hurry, so that it is difficult to read.
5. **sheen** /ʃiːn/ *n.* a soft smooth shiny quality.
6. **mantel** /ˈmæntl/ *n.* a shelf above a fireplace.
7. **chant** /tʃænt/ *n.* a piece of religious music sung using a very limited range of notes, or music of this type.
8. **livery stable** /ˈlivəri ˈsteibl/ a stable where horses and vehicles are kept for hire and where stabling is provided.
9. **ephemeral** /iˈfem(ə)rəl/ *adj.* lasting for only a short time.
10. **will–o'–the–wisp** person or thing that is impossible to catch or reach.
11. **discreetly** /disˈkriːtli/ *adv.* carefully and politely, showing good sense and judgment.
12. **apothecary** /əˈpɔθɪˌkeri/ *n.* person who made and sold medicines in the past.
13. **undertaker** /ˌʌndəˈteikə/ *n.* someone whose job is to make arrangements for funerals.

A Critical Writer

I. Narration and Emplotment

The writing type of Text C is Narration. Narration is story telling, presenting a sequence of real or fictional events caused and experienced by characters. These events serve as a rough material for "plot", and "emplotment" is the aesthetic processing and rearrangement of such events. In a well-plotted story, nothing is irrelevant. Everything is highly related. It is response, interaction, and opposition that make a plot out of a simple series of events. A common way of ordering the events in a plot is to present them in the order of their occurrence in time. That is called chronological plotting. However, the author may use "flashback" to interrupt the chronological order of events, to increase suspense and promote readers' participation.

II. Question for Discussion

Have a group discussion regarding Strindberg's unique emplotment of the above story. What's the function of the half sheet of paper?

III. Your Turn to Write

Use the following clues recorded on a page of a student's notebook to write a short story; or you may tell your own story by imitating the plotting techniques in Text C.

Cathy	61831000	1/3
Library	7:00 pm	1/12
Florist	61831234	2/14
Cafeteria	6:00 pm	2/20
Film	9:30 pm	2/20
David	———	4/1
Cathy / Air China CA1321	9:00 am	6/30

Pearls of Wisdom

1. To see a world in a grain of sand
   And a heaven in a wild flower,
   Hold infinity in the palm of your hand,
   And eternity in an hour.
   　　—William Blake

   一沙见世界，
   一花显天堂。
   手掌拥无限，
   须臾纳永恒。
   　　——威廉·布莱克

2. To teach how to live with uncertainty, and yet without being paralyzed by hesitation, is perhaps the chief thing that philosophy in our age can still do for those who study it.　—Bertrand Russell

Corpus-based Exercises (1)

I. Key Word: happiness

1. *Happiness* is the key word of this chapter. Below are concordance lines of *happiness* taken from a college English corpus (CEC thereafter; around 1,200,000 words in total). Which collocations of *happiness* impress you strongly?

were very happy . / To complete their	**happiness**	, they had a baby when
eagle finished he put the final seal on my	**happiness**	by saying , " Now
drome / One effective way of damaging	**happiness**	is to look at d fix
. / The second secret is realizing that	**happiness**	is a byproduct of
. Authentic love does not imply enduring	**happiness**	. I can stay during 5
ntually gave Charlie Chaplin the stable	**happiness**	it had earlier denied
ave little consequence for your long-term	**happiness**	and success . /
ed for success , it can never guarantee	**happiness**	and fulfillment . These
There is a difference between material	**happiness**	, which implies
necessary to live a life , and spiritual	**happiness**	, which implies e alto 10
may not be what will bring you maximum	**happiness**	in life . Things n
and money itself will not bring lasting	**happiness**	to most people . Man
ces , our happiness fluctuates around our	**happiness**	set point , which
ntrol . / But the opposite is true :	**happiness**	is largely under our control
ome / One effective way of destroying	**happiness**	is to look at something 15
e from broken-hearted misery to bursting	**happiness**	— too fast , A l
ms as a human condition and don't measure	**happiness**	by an absence of
ed by Stendhal . 'Beauty is the promise of	**happiness**	,' he wrote, pointing to

2. Please try to remember the following collocations and expressions of *happiness* drawn from the above concordance lines.

complete one's happiness	enduring/lasting/stable happiness
put the final seal on one's happiness	long-term happiness
guarantee happiness	short-term happiness
measure happiness by	bursting happiness
Something is the promise of happiness.	spiritual happiness
	material happiness

3. Please translate the following Chinese sentences into English using collocations and

expressions of *happiness* you have learned from Text A and the above concordance lines.

1) 对幸福最具破坏力的做法，就是看任何事都盯着其细微的缺陷不放。
_____

2) 许多人追求金钱、美貌和权力，认为这些是幸福的保障。但是，没有它们，是否就无法幸福了呢？
_____

4. Please recite the following excerpts from the corpus.

1) Happiness is largely under our control. It is a battle to be waged and not a feeling to be awaited.

2) Happiness is not what happens to us; it's about how we perceive what happens to us. It's the knack of finding a positive for every negative, and viewing a setback as a challenge. It's not wishing for what we don't have, but enjoying what we do possess.

II. Key Word: passion

1. *Passion* is another key word in this chapter. Below are concordance lines of *passion* taken from the same corpus. Which collocations and expressions of *passion* impress you? Please write them in the following blank form.

I hated compulsory education with a	passion	. I could never quite accept the
more than an occupation to me . It is a	passion	. I love to teach as a painter loves
chers have evidence that an intrinsic	passion	for one's work is a key to rising
oon everybody around will catch the	passion	from you — like a fever . /
ird's-eye view . Her excitement and	passion	for details made Michael's dreams 5
he weekend ! I hope that you find a	passion	that matches your own talents , so that
t challenge was finding a way to fit my	passion	for cooking into my healthier li
e for children . The glory of burning	passion	may well have faded , and your
w before . / A : Red Red represents	passion	and energy . Of the eight colors
less of intimacy . There is more of	passion	and less of emotion . There is more of 10
with food more evident than in our	passion	for the hamburger . There are enough
that excites a sudden and devastating	passion	at first sight) , and she gave me the
came frequent . Reading grew into a	passion	. My first serious novel was
l communications leader powered by a	passion	to invent and an unceasing com
journey that allows them to pursue their	passion	through work . / Step 1 : 15
nights and weekends to pursue her true	passion	by earning her master's degree
love her . Of course I love her with a /	passion	almost unbearable , we're closer

_____   _____
_____   _____

2. According to the above concordance lines of *passion*, can you explain the shades of meaning between the English word *passion* and the Chinese phrase 激情?

3. Please translate the following Chinese sentence into English, trying to use the collocations and expressions from the above concordance lines.

如果你热爱某项工作，你会每天竭尽全力去做，而你的热情也将像热病一样感染周围的人。

_____

4. Please recite the following excerpt from the corpus.

There is more focus on physical beauty than on inner charm. There is more of closeness and less of intimacy. There is more of passion and less of emotion. There is more of acquiring and less of sharing. There is more of opportunism and less of selflessness. In short, there is more of ME and less of US.

Chapter Two

Love

Warming up

1. Who are beauties in your eyes? List out five of them and discuss with your group why they are beautiful. Conduct your discussion according to the table below and complete it with the agreed main features of each body part.

	Females	Males
face		
eyes		
nose		
mouth		
cheekbone		
body shape		
skin		
others		

2. "Beauty is in the eye of the beholder." How much do you agree or disagree with this popular English saying? And come up with your own definition of "beauty".

Text A

Beauty

By Alain de Botton

A Critical Reader (I)

1. ① Does beauty give birth to love or does love give birth to beauty? ② Did I love Chloe because she was beautiful or was she beautiful because I loved her? ③ Surrounded by an infinite number of people, we may ask (staring at our lover while they talk on the phone or lie opposite us in the bath) why our desire has chosen to settle on this particular face, this particular mouth or nose or ear, why this curve of the neck or dimple in the cheek has come to answer so precisely to our criterion of perfection? Every one of our lovers offers different solutions to the problem of beauty, and yet succeeds in

1. What do the first three sentences have in common?

redefining our notions of attractiveness in a way that is as original and as idiosyncratic as the landscape of their face.

2. If Marsilio Ficino (1433–99) defined love as "the desire for beauty", in what ways did Chloe fulfill this desire? To listen to Chloe, in no way whatever. No amount of reassurance could persuade her that she was anything but loathsome. She insisted on finding her nose too small, her mouth too wide, her chin uninteresting, her ears too round, her eyes not green enough, her hair not wavy enough, her breasts too small, her feet too large, her hands too wide, and her wrists too narrow. She would gaze longingly at the faces in the pages of Elle and Vogue and declare that the concept of a just God was—in the light of her physical appearance—simply an <u>incoherence</u>.

3. Chloe believed that beauty could be measured according to an objective standard, one she had simply failed to reach. Without acknowledging it as such, she was resolutely attached to a Platonic concept of beauty, an aesthetic she shared with the world's fashion magazines and which fuelled a daily sense of self-loathing in front of the mirror. <u>According to Plato and the editor of *Vogue*, there exists such a thing as an ideal form of beauty, made up of a balanced relation between parts, and which earthly bodies will approximate to a greater or a lesser degree.</u> There is a mathematical basis for beauty, Plato suggested, so that the face on the front cover of a magazine is necessarily rather than coincidentally pleasing.

4. Whatever mathematical errors there were in her face, Chloe found the rest of her body even more unbalanced. Whereas I loved to watch soapy water running over her stomach and legs in the shower, whenever she looked at herself in the mirror she would invariably declare that something was "lopsided"—though quite what I never discovered. Leon Battista Alberti (1409-72) might have known better, for he believed that any beautiful body had fixed proportions which he spelt out mathematically after dividing the body of a beautiful Italian girl into six hundred units, then working out the distances from section to section. Summing up his results in his book *On Sculpture*, Alberti defined beauty as "a Harmony of all the Parts, in whatsoever Subject it appears, fitted together with such proportion and connection, that nothing could be added, diminished or altered, but for the worse". <u>But according</u>

2 What is the meaning of "incoherence"? How does the author illustrate it?

3 Do you agree with the opinion of Plato and the editor of *Vogue*?

to Chloe, however, almost anything about her body could have been added, diminished, or altered without spoiling anything that nature had not already devastated.

5. Clearly Plato and Leon Battista Alberti had neglected something in their aesthetic theories, for I found Chloe excessively beautiful. Did I like her green eyes, her dark hair, her full mouth? I hesitate to try and pin down her appeal. Discussions of physical beauty have some of the futility of debates between art historians attempting to justify the relative merits of different artists. A Van Gogh or a Gauguin? One might try to redescribe the work in language ("the lyrical intelligence of Gauguin's South Sea skies . . ." next to "the Wagnerian depth of Van Gogh's blues...") or else to elucidate technique or materials ("the Expressionist feel of Van Gogh's later years . . ." "Gauguin's Cezanne-like linearity . . ."). But what would all this do to explain why one painting grips us by the collar and another leaves us cold? The language of the eye stubbornly resists translation into the language of words.

6. It was not beauty that I could hope to describe, only my personal response to Chloe's appearance. I could simply point out where my desire had happened to settle, while allowing the possibility that others would locate comparable perfection in quite other beings. In so doing, I was forced to reject the Platonic idea of an objective criterion of beauty, siding instead with Kant's view, as expressed in his *Critique of Judgment*, that aesthetic judgments are ones "whose determining ground can be none other than subjective".

7. The way I looked at Chloe could have been compared to the famous Müller-Lyer illusion, where two lines of identical length will appear to be of different sizes according to the nature of the arrows attached at their ends. The loving way that I gazed at Chloe functioned like a pair of outward arrows, which give an ordinary line a semblance of length it might not objectively deserve.

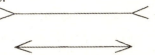

Müller-Lyer illusion

8. A definition of beauty that more accurately summed up my feelings for Chloe was delivered by

[4] Why does the author put the self-evaluation of Chloe in this way?

[5] How would you interpret the underlined sentence?

[6] What is the function of paragraph 6?

[7] What figure of speech is used here?

Stendhal. "Beauty is the promise of happiness," he wrote, pointing to the way that Chloe's face alluded to qualities that I identified with a good life: there was humour in her nose, her freckles spoke of innocence, and her teeth suggested a casual, cheeky disregard for convention. I did not see the gap between her two front teeth as an offensive deviation from an ideal arrangement, but as an indicator of psychological virtue.

8 Why does the underlined definition on beauty appear here?

A Critical Reader (II)

1. The concept of beauty usually involves both the objective standard and subjective perception for beauty. How does the author illustrate the two aspects in this essay? Please answer with specific examples.
2. The essay starts with a question "Does beauty give birth to love or does love give birth to beauty?" Has the author answered this question in the remaining part? If the author has answered the question, compare your own answer with his and share it with your group.

A Critical Writer

I. Basic Writing Techniques

1. Style and word choice

1.1 *Essays in Love*, from which Text A is taken is one of the most well-known representative works of Alain de Botton, the young British talented writer. This book narrates the story between young couples who fall in love during their journey from London to Paris, and it explores their love experience from their first kiss to fight and reconciliation, nothing unusual. But what makes this book unusual is the extent that the author goes to explore various aspects of love affairs and reveal the philosophical meaning in his witty and humorous way, which appeals to most of people who are in romantic relationships or who have just come out of such relationships. This book is characterized by a blended writing style of novel and non-fiction.

Beauty is one of the many short chapters in *Essays in Love*. In terms of the writing type of this individual chapter, it is more like a (n) _____ (A. narration B. exposition C. argumentation D. description). It explores the concept of beauty on the side of the author to his lover Chloe, and explains why Chloe is a beauty in his eyes. From his detailed analyses, the readers can clearly see the reasons why the author is attracted to Chloe who seems to be a little "ugly" ordinary woman. In order to achieve his writing purpose, the author deliberately chooses _____ (A. casual B. standard C. formal) words in his writing, which makes his words take on a pretentious appearance to leak a _____ (A. serious and convincing B. witty and humorous C. informal and friendly) sense. The high-sounding diction also attracts great attention from the readers to make them ponder on the philosophical meaning behind these words. In the end, the image of Chloe stands out with soul and flesh in front of the readers and the "beauty" of this woman becomes very convincing to the readers as well.

1.2 Replace the underlined words or phrases with the ones from the text and discuss the effects the original words or phrases can achieve.

1) Does beauty <u>cause</u> love or does love <u>cause</u> beauty?

2) Every one of our lovers <u>has different opinions</u> on beauty, and yet succeeds in redefining our ideas of attractiveness in a way that is as original and as idiosyncratic as the <u>appearance</u> of their face.

3) Discussions of physical beauty have some of the <u>useless debates</u> between art historians attempting to justify the relative merits of different artists.

4) I could simply point out where my desire had happened to settle, while <u>possibly</u> that others would locate comparable perfection in quite <u>different people</u>.

5) I did not see the gap between her two front teeth as an <u>obvious difference</u> from an ideal arrangement, but as an indicator of psychological virtue.

1.3 Eloquent writing style:

Eloquent writing style VS. Practical writing style

The style can be eloquent or practical. Eloquent style uses more abstract words, a lot of figures of speech, and the arrangement of words in sentences may have more variations than the standard word order. Practical style uses words that are concrete and specific, and the word order is usually standard.

This essay has a lot of sentences written with eloquent style. Could you find them out and change them to practical style and discuss the different effects that the two styles can achieve. An example has been made.

—We may ask (staring at our lover while they talk on the phone or lie opposite us in the bath) why our desire has chosen to settle on this particular face, this particular mouth or nose or ear…? (Paragraph 1)

—We may ask (staring at our lover while they talk on the phone or lie opposite us in the bath) why we specifically love this particular face, this particular mouth or nose or ear…?

2. Basic rules for good sentences and paragraphs

2.1 Please read Paragraph 8 again and do the following exercises:

A definition of beauty that more accurately summed up my feelings for Chloe was delivered by Stendhal. "Beauty is the promise of happiness," he wrote, pointing to the way that Chloe's face alluded to qualities that I identified with a good life: there was humor in her nose, her freckles spoke of innocence, and her teeth suggested a casual, cheeky disregard for convention. I did not see the gap between her two front teeth as an offensive deviation from an ideal arrangement, but as an indicator of psychological virtue.

1) Conciseness

Could you find any redundant words in each sentence of this paragraph?

2) Unity

What's the topic sentence of this paragraph? How are the other sentences related to the topic sentence?

3) Cohesion and Coherence

How do each sentence and the whole paragraph achieve cohesion and coherence?

2.2　Analysis:

The eighth paragraph is a good example to show how the basic qualities of good paragraphs above displayed:

1) Conciseness and Unity

There is not redundant word in each sentence. The first sentence serves as the topic sentence of this paragraph with the controlling idea that Stendhal's definition of beauty can best sum up the author's feelings towards Chloe. The remaining sentences are written around this idea. The second sentence starts with the exact definition which is followed by the specific promise of happiness that Chloe's appearance can bring to the author. In order to emphasize this idea, the author kind of repeats his explanation in the last sentence with the example of Chloe's teeth. In a word, all the three sentences are written around how the definition of beauty by Stendhal reflects the author's feelings towards Chloe.

2) Cohesion and Coherence

This paragraph displays good cohesion and coherence that is clearly shown in the relation between sentences. In the first sentence, the author projects two main ideas: one is the definition of beauty; the other is my feelings for Chloe. Then, the beginning of the second sentence is to present what such definition is, and the remaining part of the sentence is to explain what exactly my feelings are. We can see the close relationship between the first and the second sentence. Even within the second sentence itself, the second part is also to explain "Beauty is the promise of happiness". The author uses specific words to describe the happiness that Chloe's beauty brings to him, like humour, innocence, casual, disregard for convention. And the last sentence is to further such happiness by referring the gap between her front teeth to a psychological virtue.

2.3　Exercises:

1) Please read the following two pairs of sentences carefully and choose the more concise one. And find out more examples to discuss with your partner how conciseness is displayed.

☐ a. The language of the eye stubbornly resists translation into the language of words.

☐ b. The language of the eye stubbornly resists being translated into the language of words.

☐ a. It was not beauty that I could hope to describe, but what I hope to describe is my personal response to Chloe's appearance.

☐ b. It was not beauty that I could hope to describe, only my personal response to Chloe's appearance.

2) Please read the following two sentences carefully and figure out the controlling idea of each sentence. And find out more examples to discuss with your partner how unity is displayed.

a. Surrounded by an infinite number of people, we may ask (staring at our   Paragraph 1
lover while they talk on the phone or lie opposite us in the bath) why
our desire has chosen to settle on this particular face, this particular
mouth or nose or ear, why this curve of the neck or dimple in the cheek
has come to answer so precisely to our criterion of perfection?

the controlling idea:

b. In so doing, I was forced to reject the Platonic idea of an objective   Paragraph 6
criterion of beauty, siding instead with Kant's view, as expressed in
his *Critique of Judgment*, that aesthetic judgments are ones "whose
determining ground can be none other than subjective".

the controlling idea:

3) Please read the following two sentences carefully and figure out how the clear connection between different parts is achieved. And find out more examples to discuss with your partner how coherence is displayed.

a. If Marsilio Ficino (1433–99) defined love as "the desire for beauty",   Paragraph 2
in what ways did Chloe fulfill this desire?

b. Chloe believed that beauty could be measured according to an objective   Paragraph 3
standard, one she had simply failed to reach.

4) Please write a paragraph by imitating Paragraph 8 and the main body of the first sentence has been provided.

A definition of <u>love</u> that more accurately sums up my feelings for _____ is delivered by

_____

_____

_____

_____

_____

3. Basic rules for good essays: Well-organized structure

3.1 Questions:

1) How many parts can this essay be divided into, and what is the main idea for each part?

2) What is the writing thread of this essay? In what ways does it accomplish its thread function?

3.2 Analysis:

This essay is a typical exposition in which the author makes great efforts to explain his ideas towards beauty, more specially his responses to Chloe's "beauty". Any exposition is composed of three main sections: introduction, development and conclusion. Let's examine how the author has accomplished his writing purpose in each section.

Introduction

A good introduction should have an Opener, a Lead-in and a Thesis Statement. The first sentence "Does beauty give birth to love or does love give birth to beauty?" is a well-served Opener, an interesting opening sentence that catches the readers' attention and sets up the topic for discussion. And then the following two sentences "Did I love Chloe because she was beautiful or was she beautiful because I loved her? Surrounded by an infinite number of people, we may ask (staring at our lover while they talk on the phone or lie opposite us in the bath) why our desire has chosen to settle on this particular face, this particular mouth or nose or ear, why this curve of the neck or dimple in the cheek has come to answer so precisely to our criterion of perfection?" guide the readers from the broad, general topic to the narrow, relevant issue, the relationship between my love to Chloe and her appearance. This is how Lead-in works. The last sentence presents a specific statement of the author's position on the issue and provides the framework for the essay. The entire essay must focus on proving this point.

Development

The development section is the body of the essay. In this section, the author fully develops its content. The paragraphs 2, 3, 4 and 5 constitute the first part of the development section. In this part, the author argues with several conventional ideas about love and beauty, like love is the "desire for beauty" and the golden proportion of the beauty. It seems that Chloe, his lover, satisfies none of them. While illustrating this, the author mainly uses contrast. Then, the first sentence of Paragraph 6 "It was not beauty that I could hope to describe, only my personal response to Chloe's appearance." turns the discussion to the second part which explains Chloe's appearance in the author's eyes. Different from the conventional ideas, the author's ideas about their love and Chloe's beauty becomes clearer and clearer through detailed explanation.

Conclusion

A good conclusion should not only provide a sense of closure, but also return the readers to the opening theme of the essay. In the last paragraph, the author refers to a definition of beauty to summarize his responses to Chloe's beauty in detail. It actually well answers the question asked in the introduction section. "Does beauty give birth to love or does love give birth to beauty?" Chloe's beauty gives birth to the author's love and the author's love also gives birth to her beauty.

3.3 Working out an outline:

Please work out a writing plan on the topic Love according to the analysis above. Your

writing plan should address at least the following questions:
1) How many parts are there in your writing?
2) What is the main idea for each part?
3) What examples or writing strategy will you use for each part?

II. Specific Writing Techniques

1. Parallelism
Parallelism means giving two or more parts of the sentences a similar form so as to give the whole a definite pattern. As a rhetorical device, parallelism can arouse the readers' attention and give the language a sound-pleasing rhyme.

Exercise: Could you find out the parallel sentences and discuss the effects that such sentence pattern can achieve?

2. Writing imitation:
In paragraph 2, the author described Chloe's appearance in great detail to show how her appearance is against the definition on love suggested by Marsilio Ficino (1433–99). But after reading the whole essay, we get to know that the author, Alain de Botton, has quite different idea on love and Chloe's appearance, could you write a similarly structured paragraph to show Alain de Botton's point of view.

If Marsilio Ficino (1433—99) defined love as "the desire for beauty", in what ways did Chloe fulfill this desire? To listen to Chloe, in no way whatever. No amount of reassurance could persuade her that she was anything but loathsome. She insisted on finding her nose too small, her mouth too wide, her chin uninteresting, her ears too round, her eyes not green enough, her hair not wavy enough, her breasts too small, her feet too large, her hands too wide, and her wrists too narrow. She would gaze longingly at the faces in the pages of Elle and Vogue and declare that the concept of a just God was—in the light of her physical appearance—simply an incoherence.

If Alain de Botton defined love as _____, in what ways did Chloe fulfill this _____? To listen to Alain, in every way. _____. He insisted on finding her nose _____, her mouth_____ , her chin _____, her ears _____, her eyes____ _____, her hair _____, her breasts _____, her feet ___, her hands _____, and her wrists _____. He would _____.

III. Your Turn to Write

Please write an essay on the topic "Love" with the outline you have worked out. Besides, try to use what you have learned and exercised on lexical, syntactic and discourse levels.

Pearls of Wisdom

1. Though we travel the world over to find the beautiful, we must carry it with us or we find it not.   —Ralph Waldo Emerson

2. Our hearts are drunk with a beauty our eyes could never see.   —George W. Russell

3. Some people, no matter how old they get, never lose their beauty—they merely move it from their faces into their hearts. —Martin Buxbaum

Text B

Warming up

1 How often do you go home? On your way home, how do you usually feel?
2 How important does going home mean to you? Why?

Going Home

By Pete Hamill

I first heard this story a few years ago from a girl I had met in New York's Greenwich Village. Probably the story is one of those mysterious bits of folklore that reappear every few year, to be told anew in one form or another. However, I still like to think that it really did happen, somewhere, sometime.

1. They were going to Fort Lauderdale—three boys and three girls—and when they boarded the bus, they were carrying sandwiches and wine in paper bags, dreaming of golden beaches and sea tides as the gray, cold spring of New York vanished behind them.

2. As the bus passed through New Jersey, they began to notice Vingo. He sat in front of them, dressed in a plain, ill-fitting suit, never moving, his dusty face masking his age. He kept chewing the inside of his lip a lot, frozen into complete silence.

3. Deep into the night, outside Washington, the bus pulled into Howard Johnson's, and everybody got off

A Critical Reader

1 What can you tell from the description of Vingo here?

except Vingo. He sat rooted in his seat, and the young people began to wonder about him, trying to imagine his life: perhaps he was a sea captain, a runaway from his wife, an old soldier going home. When they went back to the bus, one of the girls sat beside him and introduced herself.

4. "We're going to Florida," she said brightly. "I hear it's really beautiful."

5. "It is," he said quietly, as if remembering something he had tried to forget.

6. "Want some wine?" she said. He smiled and took a swig from the bottle. He thanked her and retreated again into his silence. After a while, she went back to the others, and Vingo nodded in sleep.

7. In the morning, they awoke outside another Howard Johnson's, and this time Vingo went in. The girl insisted that he join them. He seemed very shy, and ordered black coffee and smoked nervously as the young people chattered about sleeping on beaches. When they returned to the bus, the girl sat with Vingo again, and after a while, slowly and painfully, he began to tell his story. He had been in jail in New York for the past four years, and now he was going home.

8. "Are you married?"

9. "I don't know."

10. "You don't know?" she said.

11. "Well, when I was in jail I wrote to my wife," he said. "I told her that I was going to be away a long time, and that if she couldn't stand it, if the kids kept askin' questions, if it hurt her too much, well, she could just forget me. I'd understand. Get a new guy, I said—she's a wonderful woman, really something—and forget about me. I told her she didn't have to write me. And she didn't. Not for three and a half years."

12. "And you're going home now, not knowing?"

13. "Yeah," he said shyly. "Well, last week, when I was sure the parole was coming through, I wrote her again. We used to live in Brunswick, just before Jacksonville, and there's a big oak tree just as you come into town. I told her that if she didn't have a new guy and if she'd take me back, she should put a yellow handkerchief on the tree, and I'd get off and come home. If she didn't want me, forget it—no handkerchief, and I'd go on through."

2 What are the possible reasons for such an answer to the question "Are you married"?

14. "Wow," the girl exclaimed. "Wow."

15. She told the others, and soon all of them were in it, caught up in the approach of Brunswick, looking at the pictures Vingo showed them of his wife and three children—the woman handsome in a plain way, the children still unformed in the much-handled snapshots.

16. Now they were 20 miles from Brunswick, and the young people took over window seats on the right side, waiting for the approach of the great oak tree. Vingo stopped looking, tightening his face, as if fortifying himself against still another disappointment.

17. Then Brunswick was 10 miles, and then five. Then, suddenly, all of the young people were up out of their seats, screaming and shouting and crying, doing small dances of joy. All except Vingo.

18. Vingo sat there stunned, looking at the oak tree. It was covered with yellow handkerchiefs—20 of them, 30 of them, maybe hundreds, a tree that stood like a banner of welcome billowing in the wind. As the young people shouted, the old con slowly rose from his seat and made his way to the front of the bus to go home.

[3] Why did the girl exclaim "Wow"?

[4] What might Vingo be thinking about while getting closer home?

A Critical Reader (II)

[1] What does going home mean to Vingo?
[2] Which part of the story impresses you most? Why?
[3] What is the symbolic meaning of the yellow handkerchief?

A Critical Writer

I. Style and Word Choice

1. Characterization is one of the important elements of narrative. Careful word choice can definitely contribute to the characterization. Please fill out the table below to see how the author achieves characterization in this short story.

Characters	Characteristics	Careful Word Choice
Vingo	shy, quiet, _____	
Young people	active, _____, _____	
Vingo's wife	kind, _____, _____	

2. Besides careful word choice, deliberate use of tense also helps in characterization. Try to find the different tenses used by the author when describing Vingo and the young people and discuss the different effects by filling out the table below.

Characters	Effects	Deliberate Use of Tense
Vingo		
Young people		

II. Good Structure in the Level of Paragraph and Essay

1. This essay is a typical _____(A. exposition B. narrative C. argumentation) and it can be divided into three parts. The first part, from paragraph _____ to _____, introduces the setting and main characters of the story. The second part is the development of the story, from paragraph _____ to _____ to show how the young people are getting interested in finding out the result. The climax of the story,_____, comes at the last part, from paragraph _____ to _____. The whole essay is mainly developed by (A. time B. space C. cause and effect D. compare and contrast E. examples).

2. While reading the essay, the reader cannot being attracted to find out the result. In order to achieve this, the author deliberately creates suspense during the whole process on both syntactic and discourse levels. For example:

1) They were going to Fort Lauderdale — three boys and three girls — and when they boarded the bus, they were carrying sandwiches and wine in paper bags, dreaming of golden beaches and sea tides as the gray, cold spring of New York vanished behind them.

2) As the bus passed through New Jersey, they began to notice Vingo. He sat in front of them, dressed in a plain, ill-fitting suit, never moving, his dusty face masking his age. He kept chewing the inside of his lip a lot, frozen into complete silence.

The first two paragraphs depict a sharp contrast in the behaviors between the young people and Vingo. Such contrast will arouse the readers' attention and make us think why Vingo behaves so differently and even strangely on a bus to the golden tour attraction, Florida. Then suspense comes into being and readers get caught. Could you find some other places in the essay to show the suspense created and discuss their effects?

3. Writing task:

Vingo's wife is an important hidden character of this essay. In the end, we get to know she chooses to forgive her husband and wait for him all the time. Could you write another ending paragraph for this essay? Please focus on the appearance of Vingo's wife, her way of looking at Vingo and her words said to him. And try to create some suspense too in this paragraph.

III. Your Turn to Write

Have you ever tried to forgive someone or get forgiveness from someone? Please shape your experience into a narrative with suspense, which means you should not tell the result until the end of your writing.

Pearls of Wisdom

1. Life is the first gift, love is the second, and understanding the third. —Marge Piercy

2. From where we are there is always a path toward love. What takes discipline is continually choosing that path. —Jesse Pender

3. Failure is a judgment, an opinion. It stems from your fears, which can be eliminated by love — love for yourself, love for what you do, love for others, and love for your planet. —Wayne Dyer

Text C

Cyber Love: What Is Real & What Is Virtual

By Cindy Grant

A Critical Reader

1. The conventional bar scene of the 70s and 80s is no longer the accepted place to meet prospective dates. Lately, more and more singles are turning to the Internet for better dating opportunities. Talk show hype over cyberspace love encounters and the movie *You've Got Mail* have popularized the romantic potential of the Internet. The process of an online relationship; however, is very different from real time dating processes. The online environment is, by its very nature, restrictive. For new

1 What are the differences between the online dating process and real time dating process?

Internet users, the online culture shock can be daunting.

2. Learning to communicate on the Internet is the first obstacle for newbies. Emoticons such as :-), LOL, and <G> are used liberally to express emotion, and can be like learning a foreign language. The rules are different online as well. There are protocols to follow in chat rooms; for example, to avoid accidentally offending others, sarcasm must be spelled out. Devoid of body language and intonation, the typed word is the only way to get the message across. Most novice Internet chat users first begin as "lurkers," content to quietly watch others interact. This way, the Internet culture is safely and quietly experienced before a user feels comfortable interacting within it.

❷ What is the meaning of "lurkers"?

3. Another noticeable inconvenience, especially for women, is the seemingly endless number of chatters who want casual "cyber sex." This affront discourages many new chat users from returning, and also perpetuates the image of the Internet being "dirty." These cyber sex hound-offenders are attracted to the anonymity of the Internet. Where else can they act so rudely without getting caught?

4. However, all novice chat users are mesmerized to some degree by the extreme anonymity and fantasy potential the Internet provides. Often, the user eventually realizes the sensitivity needed to interact with others—a transition is made from relating to the computer to relating to other people online. Often, this transition is coupled with an event that brings about this reality—such as "falling in love" with a fantasy and dealing with the reality that follows, meeting a chat partner face to face, or realizing that careless actions have hurt another person. Once this transition occurs, the chat user suffers a period of disillusionment, and then chooses to continue chat use—now wiser and kinder, or abandons Internet chat altogether.

❸ Why do the online users need sensitivity?

5. MIT sociology professor Sherry Turkle has extensively studied people's relationships to computers. In her book, *Life on the Screen*, Turkle defines the aspects of the self as they relate to the new Internet culture.

6. According to Turkle, "people are able to build a self by cycling through many selves" on the Internet (Turkle, 1995). This is a new phenomenon, and counters the psychoanalytic definition of identity as being forged early in life. By trying on various personas, Internet users are able to experiment with their own identity.

7. This identity experimentation, however, is not without risks and complications. While experimentation can be a healthy exploration, it can also be damaging to self-esteem. Turkle describes cases where the Internet users feel more confident as "altered selves," losing confidence in their real identity (Turkle, 1995). Often, it is the state of the self-esteem at the beginning of the experimentation that determines whether the experience is positive or negative. For example, someone who suffers from depression, will likely realize a negative impact by experimenting with his or her identity online.

8. Identity experimentation also complicates the Internet dating arena. Not all identity experimentation is intentional. Some Internet users involved in online romances describe their relationship in these terms: "I'm a different person when I'm with him [online]" or "I'm happy and confident when we are talking online. I'm not like that any other time." These feelings might be incorrectly attributed to the relationship's success, when the reality is that behavior has been altered through subconscious self-exploration. Once these relationships move off line, they often wane, since the magic (and the altering of identity) cannot be maintained without the online illusion.

9. Don't make hasty commitments. "Love at first type" is romantic, but not always realistic. Take your time and do it right. Consider free online dating web sites. Most of these are divided into major cities or geographical areas, increasing the chance of finding the right person locally. Also, because there is more of an expectation to meet in real time, there are fewer lurkers. However, as with dating services, you must contend with candidates with less-than-noble motives. Always be aware.

10. Make friends. You will certainly meet many people that aren't right for you, but they are still interesting. The Internet is a great place to make friends.

11. Meet early. Once you like someone online and they like you, progress to a real time meeting. Until you hit it off on all levels, keep your options open.

12. When you meet in real time (RT), play it safe. Remember that you are meeting a stranger. Opt for public places, such as a restaurant. Or consider bringing along a friend.

13. The Internet has its share of love and heartache. With so many people using the Internet, chances are great

4 What is identity experimentation?

5 Do you agree on the three suggestions?

that you will find your mate, provided you use common sense, a lot of patience, and a willingness to take a budding online relationship into the real world.

A Critical Writer

Exposition and Clarity

The writing type of Text C is Exposition. Exposition is to explain or explore something, such as the process of making a machine, the causes of a natural or social phenomenon, the planning of a project, or the solution of a problem[1]. This essay is to explore the new social phenomenon, cyber love. By explaining this phenomenon from different aspects, the author can arouse the readers' attention on it and get them to start thinking about it, since the phenomenon becomes more and more popular and will take up an important role in building up people's relationship.

I. Question for Discussion

Clarity is one of the most important features of exposition. In order to achieve clarity, what means does the author use?

II. Your Turn to Write

Please write on a social phenomenon that attracts your attention a lot and shape it into an exposition. The purpose of your writing is to get people to think about this social phenomenon.

Pearls of Wisdom
Chat Room Love

by Guitarplayer152
Don't even know who you are,
yet all I know is that you live really far.
You tell me all these things you say are true,
but all that does is make me want to see you.

You tell me that you look so fine
and say that someday you will be mine.
Telling me that you wish to be my wife,
always explaining how you want to help my life.

---

1 丁往道等,《英语写作手册》, 外语教学与研究出版社, 1994, 第181页。

As soon as I enter the chat room just to say hi,
you are the first person to talk to me before I say bye.
Asking questions like if I really care about you,
Waiting for my answer, I have no choice but to say I do.

When I have to leave you stop talking to me,
which makes me stay just to make you happy.
But when you go, you leave without saying goodbye,
which makes me want to logout and die.

I watch you tell other people that you love them,
and watch them call you their little gem.
But every time you say you are sorry,
I fall for it and say no need to worry.

I wish to find out who you are
and go to your house even though its far.
I want to talk to you really soon
to prove if the way I feel for you is somewhat true.

Corpus-based Exercises (2)

I. Key Word: love

Below are concordance lines of *love* taken from a corpus of college English texts.

f living For some a way to feel And some say	love	is holding on And some say let it
ding on And some say let it go And some say	love	is everything Some say they
omes together with its share of sadness .	love	/ Given the busy nature of our
iend . / I somehow grew up believing that	love	would happen when it had to .
ds a lot of give and not so much of take . /	love	was a magnificent building I 5
al school of romance , But in my opinion ,	love	needs to be nurtured . And it has
nguished from the intense but short-lived	love	or the pleasures of the flesh . /
how managed to help preserve the holiness of	love	and relationships . / The
roximity , has jumped on the bandwagon of	love	with so much haste that it is
everything that can make us stronger . True	love	happens once in a lifetime . 10
- I felt pure and honest expressions of his	love	? / In those hands , also ,
was the time my father chose to show his	love	for the special people in his

package at my chair . The card was signed "	love	, Dad , " and the gift was a
and always included a special card signed "	love	, Dad . " In those years my
d gifts from " significant others " , and "	love	Dad " just didn't seem quite	15
h it , in barely legible handwriting , was "	love	, Dad . " / His final card
I had a father who continued a tradition of	love	with a generosity of spirit ,
hoes , whatever . Then you buy it and you	LOVE	having it for a few days .
use , well-raised children , a home built on	love	, a clear conscience , a
onditional on such things as excitement ,	love	, popularity and whether that	20
e things that bring profound joy — birth ,	love	, marriage — also bring
ring responsibility and the risk of loss .	love	may not last , sex isn't
t an uninterrupted morning writing , which I	love	. When the kids came
rt disease because they believe they are in	love	. But HIV is different . And
use cooking was how my mother expressed her	love	, her pride , her power , her	25
than ten years ago when Tonya Verbeek fell in	love	with wrestling . But in the

1. Three sentences from above have been listed out. You may choose to either counter argue with it or support it with another sentence. Please learn from the sentence and try to make your own concise and meaningful.

1) Some say love is holding on and some say let it go.

2) True love happens once in a lifetime.

3) I somehow grew up believing that love would happen when it had to.

2. Some of the sentences are full of profound meaning and thought-provoking, but they are not completely displayed. Could you complete the sentence according to the context?

1) Some say love is everything. Some say they don't know ...

2) Love may not last, sex isn't always good, ...

3) ...be distinguished from the intense but short-lived love or the pleasures of the flesh.

II. Key Word: commitment

Below are concordance lines of *commitment* taken from a corpus of college English texts.

lent way to express affection and	commitment	. But if you insist that yo
both partners and renews their	commitment	to each other . It gives th

oday, Dr. King's legacy — the	**commitment**	to take affirmative action	
emia. They haven't really made a	**commitment**	to being an academic sta	
utifully reiterated his patriotic	**commitment**	to play for the national te	5
o many times, the idea of a lifetime	**commitment**	to a certain job seems	
ome demonstration of altruistic	**commitment**	, such as medicine. /	
selves — our children. Dubbed "	**Commitment**	2000," its objective is t	
ot deserve support for making this	**commitment**	.I only mean to point	
om study; it requires much time,	**commitment**	and discipline to ke	10
ence. This usually requires extra	**commitment**	by these students. Whet	
s normally sequential and requires	**commitment**	on the students' part. Ke	
ns remain as to its true level of	**commitment**	/ Eastern Europe /	
and their working long hours as	**commitment**	to the company. Of cour	
there is nothing wrong with their	**commitment**	, ambition and dura	15
tes attend four-year colleges. /	**Commitment**	among parents is a key in	
mistic that once parents make a	**commitment**	to the program, they wil	
and carries a heavier burden of	**commitment**	. / But as we use the	

1. Study the following list of *commitment* collocations drawn from the above concordance lines.

a lifetime commitment	express affection and commitment	burden of commitment
altruistic commitment	make a commitment to being	level of commitment
extra commitment	renew their commitment to each other	
patriotic commitment	require commitment on one's part	

2. Please paraphrase the underlined phrases of *commitment*.

1) It is also true of the <u>world's collective commitment</u> to the architecture of globalization.

_____

2) The official said the meeting would give ministers the chance to <u>affirm a commitment to free</u> trade and to discuss reforming financial institutions.

_____

3) The rationale was that the Army needs to get bigger in order to <u>sustain a long-term commitment</u> in Iraq and Afghanistan without wearing out the troops and alienating their families.

_____

Chapter Three

Family

Warming up

It is universally believed that the most reliable and true relationship is the one that a person has with his family. Family plays such an important role in one's life that it can help form one's view of thinking and understanding of the world. Please describe your own family to your partners and talk about how your family shapes your personality and character.

① Are there some traditions in your family?
② Do you think it necessary to keep them and pass them down?
③ How is your relationship with your family now?
④ What's the perfect family mode in your mind?

Text A

The Lost Art of Family Traditions

By Ralph Nader

A Critical Reader (I)

1. They are free, valuable, personal and too often not mentioned or used. I speak of the insights, wisdom and experiences of families over several generations. Now that Thanksgiving weekend is over, how many families recounted some of their traditions for their children and grandchildren to absorb and enjoy? It is highly probable that electronic toys, music and videos received more than a little attention over those four days.

2. That is a problem. Many youngsters are spending about 50 hours a week watching screens—television, video and computer—for the most part as spectators or engaged in trivial pursuits such as endless text messaging or fiddling with[1] their Facebook profile.

3. Yet in the overall picture of family upbringing, it is what families do together, participate with one another

[1] According to the author, what's the value of family traditions? Are they still observed in current families? What do young people do in family days?

[2] What's the structural function of Paragraph 3?

and their friends or relatives in their neighborhood that significantly shape character and personality.

4. Earlier this year, I wrote a book called THE SEVENTEEN TRADITIONS about how my mother and father raised their four children in a small factory town in Connecticut during the Thirties, Forties and Fifties. The seventeen traditions marked the ways we were raised-learning to listen, how to think independently, how to learn from history and from our siblings, how to work, care for our community, respect our parents and relish simple enjoyments needing our engagement, for example.

5. The reaction to this book from around the country was uniformly positive, making this the only book I have written that everyone loves. Why? Besides the helpful sayings and problem-solving ways of my parents (such as getting us to eat right) the book was well received because these pages often resonated with[2] their own family memories and made people more aware of their great-grandparents, grandparents and parents at their best.

3 Does this paragraph whip up any interesting stories or proverbs your grandparents or great-grandparents told you in your childhood? Can you share some with us?

6. Sadly, the transmission of these best sayings, insights and experiences are not being set down, notwithstanding the plethora of[3] recording equipment. Pictures galore[4], yes. But my sense in speaking with hundreds of people, during my book tour is that recognition of these family gems is not often accompanied by their being written or recorded for transmission to the next generations. It is too easy to procrastinate[5] and then, suddenly it is too late for granny or grandpa and this priceless inheritance is lost forever to the children and grandchildren.

4 Why are the family traditions not passed down?

7. Coming from the forebears or ancestors, these traditions mean a great deal for these youngsters and even more when they grow older. The same wisdom, song, poetry, proverb (my parents disciplined us with proverbs, not believing in corporal punishment) coming from other sources is just not as memorable, repeatable or meaningful. Mother and father raised two girls and two boys who enjoyed civic activity. They taught us the tradition of civics and how to form our civic personality of resilience[6] and critical thinking by the force of their own example. They regularly participated in community activities enhancing justice, safety (eg. from floods) and charity. Today, the commercialization of childhood by hundreds of companies saturating[7] children directly with advertisements for

5 How does the author himself acquire resilience and critical thinking? Does he think children nowadays have the same chance? Why?

things and programs which are generally not good for them—junk food, violent and salacious[8] programming and so forth—has undermined parental authority and taken advantage of the days when parents are away commuting to and from work. Yet, it is the family structure which is indispensable to a strong, self-confident people that relates to community and work with a resourcefulness that places important civic values over the relentless drive for profits or commercial values.

8. Every major religion many centuries ago warned its adherents not to give too much power to the merchant classes. The stomping[9] on other societal values by powerful greed caught the attention of the early prophets more through daily observation than through revelation.

9. For some months, we have asked families all over the country to send us a tradition or two—an insight or experience—to get the ball rolling for preserving their own family collection. The website for such examples is seventeentraditions.com. Joy wrote us recalling that during the 1960s and 1970s, she and her husband had a rule for their daughter that "she could not have anything she had seen advertised on TV, because the price of an advertised product would be inflated to pay for the advertising that made her want it in the first place.... The lesson was one of both cost-consciousness and awareness of advertising manipulation."

10. As a teaching prod and a discussion starter, this tradition of Joy's family came filled with thought-provoking, peer group resistant, health advancing benefits. The vast majority of products advertised for children on television are easily avoidable or replaceable once critically appraised. So, send us a "best practice" or a penetrating insight from your family history for placement on seventeentraditions.com. Have this holiday season be the occasion for starting up these wonderful and helpful recollections to enrich and protect the family from the corrosive and damaging predatory[10] forces which surround families from so many directions.

11. In the book, I recount one day when, at age ten, I came home from classes and my father asked me: "Well, Ralph, what did you learn in school today, did you learn how to believe or did you learn how to think?"

12. Need more be said?

6 How is the author's idea unfolded in this paragraph?

7 From Paragraph 7 and 8, can you figure out what the author's opinion towards commercials is? Why?

8 Do you agree with Joy's family rule mentioned in Paragraph 9? Do you think it feasible?

9 Why does the author mention his father asking him after school one day at ten at the very ending of the essay?

Notes

1. **fiddle with** keep moving or touching something with one's fingers
2. **resonate with** remind somebody with something
3. **the plethora of** a large amount of something
4. **galore** /gə'lɔː/ *adj.* (something you like) existing in a very large quantities
5. **procrastinate:** /proˈkræstənet/ *v.* keep postponing something you should do because you do not want to do them
6. **resilience** /rɪˈzɪljəns/ *n.* being strong and not easily damaged
7. **saturate** /ˈsætʃəˌret/ *v.* fill a place or object completely so that no more can be added
8. **salacious** /səˈleʃəs/ *adj.* dealing with sexual matters in an unnecessarily detailed way
9. **stomp** /stɔmp/ *v.* walk with very heavy steps often because you are angry
10. **predatory:** /ˈprɛdəˌtɔri/ *adj.* eager to gain something out of someone else's weakness or suffering

A Critical Reader (II)

1. What does the author argue for?
2. Why does he hold this opinion?
3. Do you agree with him?
4. In the warming-up section, you must have talked about the significance of family to one's mental development and the tradition changes in generation transmission. Compare your idea with the author's and see whether the situation in China is different from that in America.

A Critical Writer

I. Basic Writing Techniques

1. Basic rules for good sentences and paragraphs

In Chapter 1, we have learned that a good paragraph should take on at least three traits: **coherence/cohesion, conciseness** and **unity**. Coherence/cohesion means clear *c*_____ between parts. Conciseness means no *r*_____ words. Unity in a paragraph means there is a central theme conveyed in a *t*_____ sentence and all the rest sentences relate to and support it. These three traits ensure the whole paragraph unfolded logically and in a good transition.

1.1 Read Paragraph 9 again and examine how cohesion/coherence is realized.

For some months, we have asked families all over the country to send us a tradition or two—an insight or experience—to get the ball rolling for preserving their own family collection. The website for such examples is seventeentraditions. com. Joy wrote us recalling that during the 1960s and 1970s, she and her husband had a rule for their daughter that "she could not have anything she had seen advertised on TV, because the price of an advertised product would be inflated to pay for the advertising that made her want it in the first place.... The lesson was one of both cost-consciousness and awareness of advertising manipulation."

1.2 Analysis:

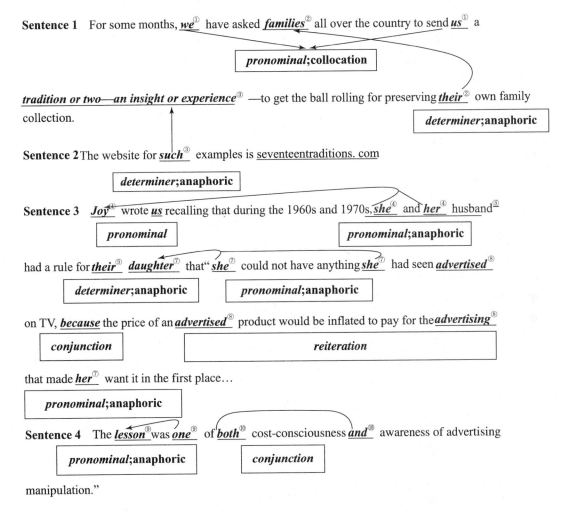

1.3 Exercises:

Read the following paragraph. How do you feel about it? Revise it, crossing the redundant words and putting it in a right order according to coherence and cohesion.

It's been said that trust is a requirement for all fulfilling relationships, whether it is in your personal life, social life, or professional life. Trust your family. When every family member understands this, you will all enjoy working and playing together. If you have respect for an individual and spend enough time with them to know their needs and desires, a mutual trust grows naturally. Learn to give things as well as take things. Successful families know and understand the importance of the "two way street" that should exist within the family structure. Every family member should know their role and understand their role and work to give things and take things on an equal basis. Trust is necessary to have open and honest relationships in the family.

1.4 Read Paragraph 7 again and do the following exercises:

(1) Coming from the forebears or ancestors, these traditions mean a great deal for these youngsters and even more when they grow older. (2) The same wisdom, song, poetry, proverb (my parents disciplined us with proverbs, not believing in corporal punishment) coming from other sources is just not as memorable, repeatable or meaningful. (3) Mother and father raised two girls and two boys who enjoyed civic activity. (4) They taught us the tradition of civics and how to form our civic personality of resilience and critical thinking by the force of their own example. (5) They regularly participated in community activities enhancing justice, safety (eg. from floods) and charity. (6) Today, the commercialization of childhood by hundreds of companies saturating children directly with advertisements for things and programs which are generally not good for them—junk food, violent and salacious programming and so forth—has undermined parental authority and taken advantage of the days when parents are away commuting to and from work. (7) Yet, it is the family structure which is indispensable to a strong, self-confident people that relates to community and work with a resourcefulness that places important civic values over the relentless drive for profits or commercial values.

Now based on the review, answer the questions below.

1) What is the central theme of the paragraph? Which sentence serves as the topic sentence?
2) How do the rest sentences relate to and support the topic sentence?
3) Can you figure out the logical structure of the paragraph?

1.5 Analysis:

In **Paragraph 7**, we can easily see how unity is achieved.

The topic sentence in this paragraph is **Sentence (1)**, expressing the central theme that family traditions are valuable for all people, young and old.

Sentence (2) is the further extension of the topic sentence, making clear what these family traditions refer to: wisdom, song, poetry and proverb coming from the forebears.

Sentence (3—5) and **Sentence (6)** are the supporting part to the topic sentence.

In **Sentence (3—5)**, the author proves the value of the family traditions by recalling his own growing experience.

On the contrary, **Sentence (6)** talks about the bad effects the lack of family traditions brings to children in the current commercialized society.

Sentence (7) is the conclusion part, restating the importance of family traditions in children's cultivation.

1.6 Exercise: Imitation

Please translate the following Chinese into English, imitating the writing techniques in Paragraph 7.

1) 家庭氛围对孩子的性格成长有着极大的影响。在轻松愉悦的家庭氛围中长大的孩子往往自信开朗；相反，在紧张压抑的家庭氛围中长大的孩子则常常缺乏自信和安全感。因此，保持良好的家庭氛围非常重要。

_____
_____
_____
_____

2) 父母的行为模式可以影响子女的行为模式。如果父母处事端方，子女多诚实质朴；相反，如果父母行止有失，子女身上就会出现撒谎等行为。因此，在教育子女的同时，父母一定要多反省自己的行为。

_____
_____
_____
_____

3) 家庭成员间的关系是否紧密可以解释子女成年后的人际关系情况。如果……；相反，如果……。因此，……。（请根据主题句补全省略处）

_____
_____
_____
_____

2. Basic rules for good essays: Well-organized structure

A column essay, as we have learnt, expresses the author's opinion towards a social phenomenon. It belongs to the category of argumentative essays.

The part of Introduction serves to make clear what issue the essay is going to talk about, and more importantly, the **thesis statement** which clarifies the author's opinion towards the issue. To some extent, the function of thesis statement in an argumentative essay is like that of the topic sentence in a paragraph, both revealing the central theme of the whole unit.

The part of Body functions to support the thesis statement, that is, to provide reasons or evidence why the author holds the opinion. In this part, one can enumerate examples plus for one's stand, or compare and contrast the possible situation caused by the opposite extremes, or explain to some detail why one holds the point.

The part of Conclusion is the summary of the essay. In this part, the supporting details are brought to an end and the thesis statement is emphasized. To emphasize the thesis statement, one can restate it in other words, or pose a question or story connected to it so as to provoke the reader's further thoughts, or to put up a warning. But no matter how one ends the essay, no new point should be introduced.

2.1 Questions:
1) Which sentence is the thesis statement of the essay?
2) How does the author support his thesis statement?
3) In what way is the essay ended? Does it leave you a deep impression?

2.2 Analysis:

This essay is a good example to see how introduction, body and conclusion work together to complete the writer's persuasion.

Paragraph (1—2) serve as the introduction of the essay, making the readers know that the essay is going to talk about family traditions and why the author wants to talk about it.

Paragraph (3) is the thesis statement of the essay, in which the author makes his argument clear that family traditions play such an important role in shaping one's personality and character that they should be kept and passed down.

Paragraph (4—10) is supporting details of the thesis statement.

Paragraph (4—6) can be viewed as a cluster, where the author supports his argument by pointing out the popularity of his book and the urgency most people feel to restore these family traditions.

In **Paragraph (7)**, the author supports his argument by contrasting his own growing experience and the current commercialized children cultivation. He concludes that without the guidance of family traditions, children in current society cannot acquire civic personalities like justice as naturally and effectively as he can.

In **Paragraph (8)**, the author continues to support his argument from the perspective of religion.

In **Paragraph (9—10)**, other people's family cultivation is mentioned to support the significance of family traditions.

Paragraph (11—12) is the conclusion part of the essay, where the author emphasizes his argument by one of his childhood memories and a question. Such a way to end the essay is very impressive in that the reader once more has a vivid understanding of the family tradition and sees directly its value. The last question is a rhetorical question, making the ending more powerful.

2.3 Working out an outline

Please work out an outline on the topic "Family Traditions in China" according to the analysis above. You may resort to the "Writing Process" in the Introduction of this book. Your writing plan should address at least the following questions:

1) How many parts and paragraphs do you plan to write?
2) What is the main idea for each paragraph?
3) What kind of details will you use to illustrate your point?

2.4 Exercise: Rewriting

In this essay, the writer calls for attention on the lost art of family traditions. In Paragraph 7, to promote the importance of family tradition to children cultivation, he contrasts two ways of family education, the traditional one and the current one. In the warming-up part, you and your partner have discussed family traditions in China. What traditions have been lost and do you think them worth keeping? Why do you think so? Please rewrite Paragraph 7 and contrast two opinions.

Coming from the forebears or ancestors, these traditions _____ for these youngsters and even more when they grow older. The same _____ coming from other sources is _____. Mother and father taught us the tradition of _____
_____. They _____
_____. Today, _____
_____ saturating children directly with _____
_____ which are generally not good for them—_____
_____—has undermined _____ and taken advantage of
_____. Yet, it is _____ which is indispensable
to _____.

II. Your Turn to Write

Please write an essay on the topic about the family traditions in China, whether they are kept and passed down well, or they are gradually forgotten by people. If they have been abandoned, do you think it is worthy of restoring them? Why or why not? Please pay attention to your words choice, the structures of sentences and the logical construction of paragraphs and the essay.

Pearls of Wisdom

1. Be it ever so humble, there is no place like home. —John Howard Payne
2. Happy are the families where the government of parents is the reign of affection, and obedience of the children the submission to love.—Francis Bacon

3. He is the happiest, be he King or peasant, who finds peace in his home.
—Johann Wolfgang von Goethe

Text B

Warming up

1. In your family are members closely tied to each other?
2. In real life it is often heard that in many families in-laws usually cannot get along and the relationship between mother- and daughter-in-laws as most TV shows depict is especially tense. Have you ever thought about the reason? Can you propose advice to smooth it?
3. The following text is an expository essay teaching how to build a happy and healthy family. Hope you can get some inspiration after reading it.

Building a Happy, Healthy Family

1. What a joy it is to feel harmony in our home! Striving to build a happy, healthy family is a very important endeavor[1] and the rewards are great for those who make it a priority. Families provide each of us with a sense that we belong and our families contribute to our individual identity.

2. A healthy family structure can provide the emotional support to nurture and instill a sense of security in all of us. Relationships that we share in the family also allow us to develop the morals and basic values that we carry throughout our lives. This is why it's so important that we each strive to have the goal of building a happy, healthy family. Building solid relationships within the family is absolutely essential for the success of each individual in the family, whether young or old.

3. All too often, you hear stories of dysfunctional[2] families who have multiple problems and just don't know how to function or communicate with each other. Surely this is not a scenario you imagined when you started

A Critical Reader (I)

1. What is the significance of family to individuals?

2. What is the structural function of this paragraph?

your family! Rather than risk that path in life, there are some things you can do to develop a strong family bond.

4. Respect your family members. When it comes to family members, respect should be issued from the beginning, even if it has yet to be earned. At the same time, it's also important that you work to earn the respect of other members of the family. Respect is simply the process of placing value in the other people who make up your family. Enjoy shared experiences together. The old saying, "A family who plays together stays together," is very relevant in today's world. Sharing experiences helps to build respect. It also enables you to learn more about the people that you share a home with so you can discover their likes, dislikes and the things that make them thrive from day to day. Families should work hard to ensure that they make time to spend with each other, both as a team and with each other on a one-to-one basis.

5. Trust your family. It's been said that trust is a requirement for all fulfilling relationships, whether in your personal life, social life, or professional life. If you have respect for an individual and spend enough time with them to know their needs and desires, a mutual trust grows naturally. Trust is necessary to have open and honest relationships in the family. Learn to give as well as take. Successful families know and understand the importance of the "two way street" that should exist within the family structure. When every family member understands this, you will all enjoy working and playing together. Every family member should know and understand their role and work to give and take on an equal basis.

6. If you currently have discord[3] and contention in your family, you might think it's too late to rectify the situation. However, by taking positive steps to make changes as a whole family, you can start to rebuild your trust and respect.

7. One parent alone can't make these changes by themselves. Open communication is critical so the entire family can understand what the current problems are and how to fix them. You may meet some resistance, but focusing on peace and harmony in the family should motivate even the most stubborn child. Once your family members get a taste of the happiness and security that a loving family brings to them, they won't want to live any other way!

3 How can one earn respect from other family members?

4 How can one build respect for other family members?

5 What does it mean by "two way street"?

6 How is the essay ended?

Notes

1. **endeavor** /inˈdevə/ *n.* an attempt to do something
2. **dysfunctional** /disˈfʌŋkʃənəl/ *adj.* different from what is considered normal
3. **discord** /disˈkɔ:d/ *n.* disagreement and argument between people

A Critical Reader (II)

1 Do you have a happy and harmonious relationship with your family members? What do you think is the most important factor in building a happy and healthy family?

2 Do you think the author's suggestions useful? Besides respect and trust, do you have anything else to add?

A Critical Writer

I. Basic Writing Techniques

1. Style and word choice

This is an **expository essay**. Unlike argumentative essays, expository essays are not to argue with opponents, but to teach, to give instructions, or to provide guidance. Therefore, the style and word choice of an expository is usually _____ (a. objective, b. subjective) and _____ (a. emotional b. unemotional).

2. Basic rules for good sentences and paragraphs

This is a successful essay giving us instructions of how _____. In the Introduction part (Paragraph _____), there is a natural lead into the subject and a clear thesis statement: _____. From this part, we can easily know the writer wants to tell us _____.

In the Body (Paragraph _____), the writer offers _____ ways to deal with the issue: _____ and _____.

Finally, in the Conclusion part (Paragraph _____), the writer ends the essay by _____ (A. warning, B. encouraging C. teaching D. proving) to _____ and tips to overcome difficulties in the process.

II. Specific Writing Techniques

1. Figure of speech: loose and periodic sentences

It is easy to detect that the same meaning or idea can be construed by different sentence structures. If we construe it into a loose sentence, it means we put the main idea before supplementary information so that the reader can quickly know what the sentence mainly is about as soon as he reads its first part. By contrast, if we construe the same idea into a periodic sentence, it means we express the main idea after the supplementary sentence and so the reader will not know what the sentence is mainly about until he finishes the whole part of it. For example,

1) Rather than risk that path in life, there are some things you can do to develop a strong family bond. (Paragraph 3)

2) There are some things you can do to develop a strong family bond, rather than risk that path in life.

Sentence (a) and (b) above construe the same idea. Sentence (a) is a periodic sentence, for the reader has to finish reading the whole sentence before figuring out what it is mainly about; Sentence (b), though containing the same information, is a loose sentence, because the reader can get its main idea without finishing reading it.

Loose and periodic sentences are picked according to different contexts. When one has no special emphasis among ideas but just to express them of equal importance, one should choose loose sentence; when one wants to make one of the ideas more prominent than others so as to create a suspense or climax in expression, one should choose periodic sentence.

Loose sentences are more natural and direct; periodic sentences are more formal or literal. Therefore, loose sentences are more likely utilized in informal writings, like stories, personal letters; and periodic sentences more frequently appear in formal writings, like legal documents. But there is no writing that only contains one type of sentences.

2. Exercises:

2.1 Find typical loose/periodic sentences in the essay and discuss why the information is construed in this way.

1) _____
2) _____
3) _____

2.2 Interchange following loose and periodic sentences.

1) Families provide each of us with a sense that we belong and our families contribute to our individual identity.

_____

2) When every family member understands this, you will all enjoy working and playing together.

_____

3) It has been said that trust is a requirement for all fulfilling relationships, whether in your personal life, social life, or professional life.

III. Your Turn to Write

Have you ever noticed any differences between the roles men and women play in the family? Do the differences become more or fewer in modern society than in the past? Drawing from your own experiences, write an essay and talk about it.

Working outline

Introduction (Paragraph _____)
Thesis statement: _____
Body (Paragraph _____)
Supporting detail 1 (Paragraph _____): _____
Supporting detail 2 (Paragraph _____): _____
Supporting detail 3 (Paragraph _____): _____
Conclusion (which one do you choose to end your argument?) (Paragraph _____)
- ☐ restate the thesis statement
- ☐ reemphasis the thesis statement
- ☐ propose a warning

Pearls of Wisdom

1. All happy families are like one another; each unhappy family is unhappy in its own way.   —Leo Tolstoy

2. Home is the place where, when you have to go there, it has to take you in.   —Frost Robert

3. Every soil where he is well, is to a valiant man his natural country. —Masinger Philip

Text C

Of Parents and Children

By Francis Bacon

1. The joys of parents are secret; and so are their griefs and fears. They cannot utter the one; nor they will not utter the other. Children sweeten labors; but they make misfortunes more bitter. They increase the cares of life; but

A Critical Reader

1 According to Bacon, what does "children" mean to men? What

they mitigate¹ the remembrance of death. The perpetuity² by generation is common to beasts; but memory, merit, and noble works, are proper to men. And surely a man shall see the noblest works and foundations have proceeded from childless men; which have sought to express the images of their minds, where those of their bodies have failed. So the care of posterity³ is most in them, that have no posterity. They that are the first raisers of their houses, are most indulgent towards their children; beholding⁴ them as the continuance, not only of their kind, but of their work; and so both children and creatures.

2. The difference in affection, of parents towards their several children, is many times unequal; and sometimes unworthy; especially in the mothers; as Solomon says, "A wise son rejoices⁵ the father, but an ungracious son shames the mother". A man shall see, where there is a house full of children, one or two of the eldest respected, and the youngest made wantons⁶; but in the midst, some that are as it were forgotten, who many times, nevertheless, prove the best. The illiberality of parents, in allowance towards their children, is a harmful error; makes them base; acquaints them with shifts; makes them sort with mean company; and makes them surfeit⁷ more when they come to plenty. And therefore the proof is best, when men keep their authority towards the children, but not their purse. Men have a foolish manner (both parents and schoolmasters and servants) in creating and breeding an emulation between brothers, during childhood, which many times sorts to discord when they are men, and disturbs families. The Italians make little difference between children, and nephews or near kinfolks; but so they be of the lump, they care not though they pass not through their own body. And, to say truth, in nature it is much a like matter; insomuch that we see a nephew sometimes resembles an uncle, or a kinsman, more than his own parent; as the blood happens. Let parents choose betimes⁸, the vocations and courses they mean their children should take; for then they are most flexible; and let them not too much apply themselves to the disposition of their children, as thinking they will take best to that, which they have most mind to. It is true, that if the affection or aptness of the children be extraordinary, then it is good not to cross it. Younger brothers are commonly fortunate, but seldom or never where the elder are disinherited.

[1] is the difference in perpetuity by generation between animals and men?

[2] What could it be like if the parents distribute unequal affection towards their several children?

[3] To avoid it, what is Bacon's suggestion?

[4] Why does Bacon mention the Italians here?

> **Notes**
>
> 1. mitigate /'mitigeit/ v. make something less unpleasant, serious, or painful
> 2. perpetuity /ˌpəːpi'tuiti/ n. being intended to last for ever
> 3. posterity /pɔ'steriti/ n. everyone who will be alive in the future
> 4. behold /bi'həuld/ v. see something
> 5. rejoice /ri'dʒɔis/ v. please about something
> 6. wanton /'wɔntən/ n. people (especially women) who behave in an immortal or immodest way
> 7. surfeit /'səːfit/ v. overeat, indulge
> 8. betimes /bi'taimz/ adv. in time

A Critical Reader (II)

1. In this essay, what does Bacon argue for/against? Do you agree with him? Why or why not?
2. How does Bacon support his idea?

A Critical Writer

I. Specific Writing Techniques

1. Antithesis and contrast

Antithesis is a figure of speech where two propositions opposite in meaning but similar in structure are put together. Antithesis is used to achieve a formal beauty in a strong contrast. For example,

A wise son rejoices his father, but an ungracious son shames his mother.

Contrast is another figure of speech where two aspects of one entity or two different entities are put together so as to emphasize the opposite properties in comparison. Different from antithesis, contrast does not have a strict restriction on the structures of the two propositions. For example:

Children sweeten labors, but they make misfortunes more bitter.

2. Exercises:

2.1 Imitation

1) A mother is not a person to lean on, but _____. (contrast)
2) _____, but to one person you may be the world. (antithesis)

3) The value of marriage is not that adults produce children but that _____. (antithesis)

2.2 Find other examples of antithesis and contrast in the essay and analyze their meaning, structure and rhetorical beauty.

1) _____
2) _____
3) _____
4) _____

II. Your Turn to Write

With the One-Child Policy pushed forwards, there is an increasingly large number of nuclear families: parents and one child. Some people say that children from nuclear families are less tolerant or forgiving than those growing up with siblings. Do you agree with it? Are you the only child in the family? If you are, do you crave for other siblings? Why or why not? Write an essay talking about these issues.

Pearls of Wisdom

1) How sharper than a serpent's tooth is to have a thankless child. —William Shakespeare

2) All I am, or can be, I owe to my angel mother. —Abraham Lincoln

3) Go where he will, the wise man is at home, his hearth the earth, his hall the azure dome. —Ralph Waldo Emerson

Corpus-based Exercises (3)

I. Key Word: family

1. *Family* is the key word of this chapter. Below are concordance lines of *family* taken from CEC. Which collocations of *family* impress you strongly?

love , peace , tolerance , fairness and	family	structure .
CFCs are a	family	of chemicals
the Prince of Wales , a longtime	family	friend , was announced in February 1984
Accustomed to a formal and stuffy royal	family	the British public was delighted.
getting married and starting a	family	

In France and Britain , breakfast is a	**family**	affair.
the wife, and four children , the extended	**family**	the hundreds and hundreds of friends who satin pain
overworked colored man with too large a	**family**	NAME?
On a	**family**	basis, the labels are sometimes attached by the neigh
the work he loves best , he faces a	**family**	conflict — and a conflict with himself. 10
he knows that he hasn't lived up to the	**family**	label and he goes through life with a sense of guilt.
happened to have been the First	**Family**	of the nation
a second big change in American	**family**	life.
it is about	**family**	Honor
In fact, this graduated into a	**family**	habit of after-dinner quizzes at the table 15
It is a testimony to the joyful pull of	**family**	that Americans saturated the air
Does the national concern about weaker	**family**	ties say less about our feelings
Beside her a Spanish-speaking	**family**	values and Asian-Confucian group loyalty
It was evidently a united and affectionate	**family**	
related to each other in the same language	**family**	such as French and Spanish 20
By living in this loving	**family**	environment, I learned to apply the complex meani
To help with the	**family**	finances, my dad had a paper route starting at age e
the poor logger trying to feed his	**family**	and pay his mortgage out in rural America…
to work to secure a living for his	**family**	
Born to a modest	**family**	in India in 1869, Gandhi studied law in London 25
she had written about this fictional	**family**	which carried a lot of different themes
Laurie came from a skating	**family**	
about the meaning of the term "good	**family**	man," many responded that it was a phrase…
men who quietly yet proudly fulfill their	**family**	responsibilities
society acts as if	**family**	obligations are not as important to fathers 30
took a month off between jobs to get his	**family**	Established
the closest thing we have to a global	**family**	Tree
a different sort of English that relates to	**family**	talk, the language I grew up with.
have the goal of building a happy , healthy	**family**	
but they are not, committed to the	**family**	circle, but they are not, as in German… 35
to develop a strong	**family**	bond. Respect your family members.

2. Please try to remember the following collocations and expressions of *family* drawn from the above concordance lines.

"family" as adjective		collocation with verbs
family structure	family name	start a family
family friend	family basis	feed one's family
family affair	family conflict	secure a living for his family
family label	family life	fulfill one's family responsibility
family evening	family honor	get one's family established
family habit	family ties	committed to the family circle
family finances	family man	graduate into a family habit
family responsibility	family obligations	live up to the family label
family talk	family circle	
family bond	family tree	

modifiers + family	collocations with prepositions
a happy, healthy family	a family of …
a skating family	the pull of family
fictional family	
a modest family	
loving family environment	
language family	
a unite and affectionate family	
a Spanish-speaking family	
First family	
The extended family	
Royal family	

3. Please translate the following Chinese sentences into English using collocations and expressions of family you have learned from Text A and the above concordance lines.

1) 他并非出身世家贵族，只是来自一个小商户家庭，因此他的脑袋中并没有家族荣誉、家族责任等概念。

2) 总体而言，我的家庭是以讲英语为主的；但是，我的祖母是没落贵族，她更喜欢讲法语；而我的母亲是移民，她更习惯讲她的母语——西班牙语。家里的早餐时间——我们的议事时间，经常是各种语言混杂的。久而久之，大家都习惯了。

3) 老话说，先成家后立业。然而在现代社会，古老的顺序已被打乱：没有事业根基的年轻人往往很难找到配偶。

4. Please recite the following excerpts from the corpus.

1) Family is, if anything, the link between generations, the center of child rearing and cultural transmission. It's not just a "big stadium" where everyone can enjoy the show. Both marriage and family involve long-term obligations and responsibility for shared care, not just the search of happiness that hollow goal of the modern age.

2) The best place to start would be in the home. Family members should practice saying such things as, "I'll wash the dishes tonight because I know you want to catch up on your thinking."

II. Key Word: insight

1. *Insight* is another key word in this chapter. Below are concordance lines of *insight* taken from the same corpus. Which collocations and expressions of *insight* impress you? Please write them in the following blank form:

This instinctive	insight	also impressed his teachers.
general principles to provide a prediction or	insight	into specific cases.
One good rule when searching for	insight	on a problem is to "sleep on it."
those three " thank you " letters gave me an	insight	into how most human beings go about
I think they must have small	insight	or great vanity. 5
my father has led me to a startling	insight	if I am still resolving my feelings about
This was no small struggling for	insight	and I was careful in my response.
The single key	insight	of Lovins' report is to focus on the need
In this way , students gain great	insight	from their peers
People are amazed at your	insight	because most are so vain they can't imag 10
argue and type their way toward	insight	
James Clerk Maxwell 's brilliant	insight	about electromagnetism
visual sightings are too unreliable to give real	insight	into its behavior.
And cam have the cultural	insight	to know when it is better to move Info
accidentally—or a sudden	insight	fitting together pieces of information 15
we can expect new	insight	into the problem of the nature of man.
The project may contribute	insight	into the old question of nature vs. nurture
his work at the university would give him	insight	into how questions of morality could be

_____   _____
_____   _____
_____   _____
_____   _____
_____   _____
_____   _____
_____   _____

2. According to the above concordance lines of passion, can you explain the shades of meaning between the English word insight and the Chinese phrase "洞察力"?

3. Please translate the following Chinese sentence into English, trying to use the collocations and expressions from the above concordance lines.

饭毕，我坐在桌前，绞尽脑汁，希望从这些只言片语中猜出说话人真正的目的。

_____

_____

4. Please recite the following excerpt from the corpus.

Insights often come when you're relaxed, when you have "turned off" your directed thinking for a while. One good rule when searching for insight on a problem is to "sleep on it." Review every aspect of the problem just before you drift off, thus guiding your unconscious to work while you sleep. In many cases, the solution will appear in a dream or will be waiting in your conscious mind when you wake up.

Friendship

> **Warming up**
>
> No one could live without friends. The one who supports you, cares about you, gives you a helping hand when you are in trouble is the most precious asset you would expect to possess. Do you have any unforgettable story about your friend? What should an ideal friend be like? Is there any difference between "friendship" and "companionship"? Does an old friend stand in the way for you to find a new friend?

Text A

Philia (selected)

By C. S. Lewis

A Critical Reader

1. Friendship arises out of mere Companionship when two or more of the companions discover that they have in common some insight or interest or even taste which the others do not share and which, till that moment, each believed to be his own unique treasure (or burden). The typical expression of opening Friendship would be something like, "What? You too? I thought I was the only one." We can imagine that among those early hunters and warriors single individuals—one in a century? One in a thousand years?—saw what others did not; saw that the deer was beautiful as well as edible, that hunting was fun as well as necessary, dreamed that his gods might be not only powerful but holy. But as long as each of these percipient persons dies without finding a kindred soul, nothing (I suspect) will come of it; art or sport or spiritual religion will not be born. It is when two such persons discover one another, when, whether with immense difficulties and semi-articulate fumblings[1] or with what would seem to us amazing and elliptical

[1] How does friendship arise from companionship?

[2] Why does the author provide the "hunter" example?

speed, they share their vision it is then that Friendship is born. And instantly they stand together in an immense solitude.

2. Lovers seek for privacy. Friends find this solitude about them, this barrier between them and the herd, whether they want it or not. They would be glad to reduce it. The first two would be glad to find a third.

3. In our own time Friendship arises in the same way. For us of course the shared activity and therefore the companionship on which Friendship supervenes will not often be a bodily one like hunting or fighting. It may be a common religion, common studies, a common profession, even a common recreation. All who share it will be our companions; but one or two or three who share something more will be our Friends. In this kind of love, as Emerson said, "Do you love me?" means "Do you see the same truth?"— Or at least, "Do you care about the same truth?" The man who agrees with us that some question, little regarded by others, is of great importance, can be our Friend. He need not agree with us about the answer.

4. Notice that Friendship thus repeats a more individual and less socially necessary level the character of the Companionship which was its matrix. The Companionship was between people who were doing something together— hunting, studying, painting or what you will. The Friends will still be doing something together, but something more inward, less widely shared and less easily defined; still hunters, but of some immaterial quarry[2]; still collaborating, but in some work the world does not, or not yet, take account of; still traveling companions, but on a different kind of journey. Hence we picture lovers face to face but Friends side by side; their eyes look ahead.

5. That is why those pathetic people who simply "want friends" can never make any. The very condition of having Friends is that we should want something else besides Friends. Where the truthful answer to the question "Do you see the same truth?" would be "I see nothing and I don't care about the truth; I only want a Friend", no Friendship can arise—though Affection of course may. There would be nothing for the Friendship to be about; and Friendship must be about something, even if it were only an enthusiasm for dominoes or white

[3] Why does the author provide the "hunter" example?

[4] How does the friendship in our own time differ from that of the primitive form?

[5] Can you give a heading to this paragraph?

[6] Why does the author suddenly mention "lovers" at the end of Paragraph 4?

[7] According to the author, what is the problem for

mice. Those who have nothing can share nothing; those who are going nowhere can have no fellow-travelers.

6. When the two people who thus discover that they are on the same secret road are of different sexes, the friendship which arises between them will very easily pass—may pass in the first half-hour—into erotic[3] love. Indeed, unless they are physically repulsive to each other or unless one or both already loves elsewhere, it is almost certain to do so sooner or later. And conversely, erotic love may lead to Friendship between the lovers. But this, so far from obliterating the distinction between the two loves, puts it in a clearer light. If one who was first, in the deep and full sense, your Friend, is then gradually or suddenly revealed as also your lover you will certainly not want to share the Beloved's erotic love with any third. But you will have no jealousy at all about sharing the Friendship. Nothing so enriches an erotic love as the discovery that the Beloved can deeply, truly and spontaneously enter into Friendship with the Friends you already had: to feel that not only are we two united by erotic love but we three or four or five are all traveler's on the same quest, have all a common vision.

7. The co-existence of Friendship and Eros may also help some moderns to realise that Friendship is in reality a love, and even as great a love as Eros. Suppose you are fortunate enough to have "fallen in love with" and married your Friend. And now suppose it possible that you were offered the choice of two futures: "Either you two will cease to be lovers but remain forever joint seekers of the same God, the same beauty, the same truth, or else, losing all that, you will retain as long as you live the raptures[4] and ardors, all the wonder and the wild desire of Eros. Choose which you please." Which should we choose? Which choice should we not regret after we had made it?

8. I have stressed the "unnecessary" character of Friendship, and this of course requires more justification than I have yet given it.

9. It could be argued that Friendships are of practical value to the Community. Every civilized religion began in a small group of friends. Mathematics effectively began when a few Greek friends got together to talk about numbers and lines and angles. What is now the Royal Society[5] was originally a few gentlemen meeting

those friendless people?

8 Can we omit the second sentence? Why?

9 What is the mutual relation between erotic love and friendship??

10 How is Paragraph 7 developed?

in their spare time to discuss things which they (and not many others) had a fancy for. What we now call "the Romantic Movement" once was Mr. Wordsworth and Mr. Coleridge talking incessantly (at least Mr. Coleridge was) about a secret vision of their own. Communism, Tractarianism, Methodism, the movement against slavery, the Reformation, the Renaissance, might perhaps be said without much exaggeration, to have begun in the same way.

11 Can we change the order in which the examples of this paragraph are arranged?

10. There is something in this. But nearly every reader would probably think some of these movements good for society and some bad. The whole list, if accepted, would tend to show, at best, that Friendship is both a possible benefactor and a possible danger to the community. And even as a benefactor it would have, not so much survival value, as what we may call "civilization value"; would be something (in Aristotelian phrase) which helps the community not to live but to live well. Survival value and civilization value coincide at some periods and in some circumstances, but not in all. What at any rate seems certain is that when Friendship bears fruit which the community can use it has to do so accidentally, as a byproduct. Religions devised for a social purpose, like Roman emperor-worship or modern attempts to sell Christianity as a means of "saving civilization", do not come to much. The little knots of Friends who turn their backs on the "World" are those who really transform it. Egyptian and Babylonian Mathematics were practical and social, pursued in the service of Agriculture and Magic. But the free Greek Mathematics, pursued by Friends as a leisure occupation, have mattered to us more.

12 What is the structural function of Paragraph 10?

11. Others again would say that Friendship is extremely useful, perhaps necessary for survival, to the individual. They could produce plenty of authority: "bare is back without brother behind it" and "there is a friend that sticketh closer than a brother". But when we speak thus we are using friend to mean "ally". In ordinary usage friend means, or should mean, more than that. A Friend will, to be sure, prove himself to be also an ally when alliance becomes necessary; will lend or give when we are in need, nurse us in sickness, stand up for us among our enemies, do what he can for our widows and orphans. But such good offices are

13 What is the topic sentence of this paragraph? How is the topic sentence introduced?

not the stuff of Friendship. The occasions for them are almost interruptions. They are in one way relevant to it, in another not. Relevant, because you would be a false friend if you would not do them when the need arose; irrelevant, because the role of benefactor always remains accidental, even a little alien, to that of Friend. It is almost embarrassing. For Friendship is utterly free from Affection's need to be needed. We are sorry that any gift or loan or night-watching should have been necessary—and now, for heaven's sake, let us forget all about it and go back to the things we really want to do or talk of together. Even gratitude is no enrichment to this love. The stereotyped[6] "Don't mention it" here expresses what we really feel. The mark of perfect Friendship is not that help will be given when the pinch comes (of course it will) but that, having been given, it makes no difference at all. It was a distraction, an anomaly. It was a horrible waste of the time, always too short, that we had together. Perhaps we had only a couple of hours in which to talk and, God bless us, twenty minutes of it has had to be devoted to affairs.

Notes

1. **fumble** /ˈfʌmbl/ *v.*   to grope awkwardly to find or to accomplish something.
2. **quarry** /ˈkwɔːri/ *n.*   hunted animals considered as a group; game.
3. **erotic** /iˈrɔtik/ *adj.*   of or concerning sexual love and desire; amatory.
4. **rapture** /ˈræptʃə/ *n.*   the state of being transported by a lofty emotion; ecstasy.
5. **Royal Society** /ˈrɔiəl səˈsaiəti/ The Royal Society of London for Improving Natural Knowledge, known as the Royal Society, is a learned society for science, and is possibly the oldest such society in existence. Founded in November 1660, it was granted a Royal Charter by King Charles II as the "Royal Society of London". The Society today acts as a scientific advisor to the British government.
6. **stereotyped** /ˈsteriəˌtaipt/ *adj.*   (of conception, opinion, or image) conventional, formulaic, and oversimplified.

A Critical Reader

1 After going through the article, what is the thesis proposed by C. S. Lewis? Do you consent to his proposition? To what extent do you approve or disapprove of his argument?

2 Try to compare/contrast your preliminary thoughts generated in the warming-up section with the argumentative points demonstrated in the article. Please structure and systemize your ideas and further bring forward more convincing counter-arguments to wrestle with the author's reasoning.

A Critical Writer

I. Basic Writing Techniques

1. Style and word choice

The Philia, C. S. Lewis' most systematic and metaphysical expounding of his insight into the essence of friendship, provides many of his pinpoint meditation which is highlighted by the distinction between friendship and companionship, erotic love and friendship and so on. In order to optimize the persuasiveness and accessibility of this particular writing, the author adopts a style that is both theoretical and practical, that is, being both authentic to serious scholastic approaches and within the range of understanding of ordinary readers at the same time. Please pay attention to the following examples selected from the text and find out how the author exercises his power of persuasion with both academic and plain words and expressions.

1) The typical expression of opening Friendship would be something like, "<u>What? You too? I thought I was the only one.</u>"

2) For us of course the shared activity and therefore the companionship on which Friendship <u>supervenes</u> will not often be a <u>bodily</u> one like hunting or fighting.

3) Notice that Friendship thus repeats a more individual and less socially necessary level the character of the Companionship which was its <u>matrix</u>.

4) There would be nothing for the Friendship to <u>be about</u>; and Friendship must <u>be about something</u>, even if it were only an enthusiasm for <u>dominoes or white mice.</u>

5) Nothing so enriches an erotic love as the discovery that the Beloved can deeply, truly and <u>spontaneously</u> enter into Friendship with the Friends you already had: to feel that not only are we two united by erotic love but we three or four or five are all traveller's on the same quest, have all a common <u>vision.</u>

6) Either you two will cease to be lovers but remain forever joint seekers of the same God, the same beauty, the same truth, or else, losing all that, you will retain as long as you live the <u>raptures and ardours,</u> all the wonder and the wild desire of Eros.

7) Relevant, because you would be a false friend if you would not do them when the need arose; irrelevant, because the role of benefactor always remains <u>accidental</u>, even a little <u>alien</u>, to that of Friend.

Please find out more of such examples by yourself.

2. Basic rules for good sentences

2.1 Unity:

Please read the following two sentences and try to find out how unity is displayed:

Sentence 1: We can imagine that among those early hunters and warriors single individuals —one in a century? One in a thousand years?—saw what others did not; saw that the deer was beautiful as well as edible, that hunting was fun as well as necessary, dreamed that his gods might be not only powerful but holy. (Paragraph 1)

Sentence 2: If one who was first, in the deep and full sense, your Friend, is then gradually or suddenly revealed as also your lover you will certainly not want to share the Beloved's erotic love with any third. (Paragraph 6)

What is the "one single, complete thought" respectively for each sentence above? And how is the "unity" actualized?

Sentence 1:

_____

Sentence 2:

_____

2.2 Cohesion and coherence:

Please read the following sentence and try to find out how cohesion and coherence is displayed:

<u>It is when</u> two such persons discover one another, when, whether with immense difficulties and semi-articulate fumblings or with what would seem to us amazing and elliptical speed, they share their vision it is then that Friendship is born. (Paragraph 1)

The Friends will still be doing something together, but something more inward, less widely shared and less easily defined; still hunters, but of some immaterial quarry; still collaborating, but in some work the world does not, or not yet, take account of; still traveling companions, but on a different kind of journey. (Paragraph 6)

Please find out more of such examples by yourself.

2.3 Conciseness: no unnecessary words.

Please convey the meaning of the following sentence in English:

1) 一旦发现你的爱人深深地、真心地、不由自主地和你的朋友建立起友谊，你们之间的爱情一定会加深，你会觉得不仅仅你们二人因为爱情走到一起，还有那么多志同道合的人出于同样的爱好和目标，都走到了一起。

_____

_____

2) 爱情和友情不同，爱情中的人感觉时时刻刻被需要，而友情不是这样。

Now please compare what you write with the text and find out how conciseness is achieved:

Nothing so enriches an erotic love as the discovery that the Beloved can deeply, truly and spontaneously enter into Friendship with the Friends you already had: to feel that not only are we two united by erotic love but we three or four or five are all traveller's on the same quest, have all a common vision. (Paragraph 6)

…

For Friendship is utterly free from Affection's need to be needed. (Paragraph 11)

Please find out more of such examples by yourself.

3. Basic rules for good paragraphs

3.1 Please read Paragraph 9 again and do the following exercises:

1) What's the topic sentence of Paragraph 9? How are the other sentences related to the topic sentence?

2) How are cohesion and coherence displayed and achieved?

3) How is the paragraph developed?

Paragraph 9

It could be argued that Friendships are of practical value to the Community. Every civilised religion began in a small group of friends. Mathematics effectively began when a few Greek friends got together to talk about numbers and lines and angles. What is now the Royal Society was originally a few gentlemen meeting in their spare time to discuss things which they (and not many others) had a fancy for. What we now call "the Romantic Movement" once was Mr. Wordsworth and Mr. Coleridge talking incessantly (at least Mr. Coleridge was) about a secret vision of their own. Communism, Tractarianism, Methodism, the movement against slavery, the Reformation, the Renaissance, might perhaps be said without much exaggeration, to have begun in the same way.

3.2 Analysis:

1) Unity:

This paragraph displays unity. The first sentence is the topic sentence of the whole paragraph with the controlling idea that "Friendships are of practical value to the Community." The rest of the paragraph, namely, from the second sentence to the last sentence, serve jointly for such a controlling idea with four prominent examples in each sentence respectively.

Sentence 1: It could be argued that Friendships are of practical value to the Community.

Sentence 2: Every civilised religion began in a small group of friends. (Religions have the practical values for soothing people's soul.)

Sentence 3: Mathematics effectively began when a few Greek friends got together to talk about numbers and lines and angles. (Mathematics has the practical value for calculating and measuring.)

Sentence 4: What is now the Royal Society was originally a few gentlemen meeting in their spare time to discuss things which they (and not many others) had a fancy for. (The Royal Society is considered as one of the most famous scientific bodies in the world, and of course, of huge practical value.)

Sentence 5—6: What we now call "the Romantic Movement" once was Mr. Wordsworth and Mr. Coleridge talking incessantly (at least Mr. Coleridge was) about a secret vision of their own. Communism, Tractarianism, Methodism, the movement against slavery, the Reformation, the Renaissance, might perhaps be said without much exaggeration, to have begun in the same way. (The Romantic Movement is of practical value for the enhancement for human's intellectual civilization.)

2) Cohesion and Coherence:

This paragraph displays cohesion and coherence, which involves both the natural development and logical connection of all the sentences. As is seen clearly from the analysis made in the section above, each sentence becomes longer than the previous one, which is direct evidence that the paragraph is developing and progressing. What should we also pay attention to is that the four examples are not arranged at random: the first two examples, the religion and Mathematics are general examples, without any specific details mentioned; the following examples contain such concrete names (Wordsworth and Coleridge) and terms (Communism, Methodism etc.). This also indicates both cohesion and coherence. The arrangement of those four sentences is open to interpretation. If you find any clue or logical line according to which those examples are arranged, please discuss it with your teachers and classmates.

3) Development:

This paragraph adopts the development by examples. What play a central role in such a development are the DETAILS. As we can easily detect, in this paragraph, details are added gradually into each sentence, thus producing not only a logic flow but also a rhythmic effect upon which a literary beauty is achieved both in its form and content. Please compare the following pairs of sentences and see what difference details can make:

Pair one:

<u>With details</u>: What is now the Royal Society was originally a few gentlemen meeting in their spare time to discuss things which they (and not many others) had a fancy for.

<u>Without details</u>: Some scientific organizations are formed because people with some common interest in something come together.

Pair two:

<u>With details</u>: What we now call "the Romantic Movement" once was Mr. Wordsworth and Mr. Coleridge talking incessantly (at least Mr. Coleridge was) about a secret vision of their own.

Without details: Some intellectual movements in human history are launched by some equally wise people who are also friends.

3.3 Writing exercise:

1) Please develop the following topic sentence into a paragraph:

The intended message presented in those printed media(also known as flat media) can be seriously distorted and biased. _____

_____

_____

_____

2) Look at the four squares [■] that indicate where the following sentence could be added to the passage.

Because the internal signals that regulate waking and going to sleep tend to align themselves with these external cues, the external clock appears to dominate the internal clock.

Animals need natural periodic signals like sunrise to maintain a cycle whose period is precisely 24 hours. ■Such an external cue not only coordinates an animal's daily rhythms with particular features of the local solar day but also—because it normally does so day after day-seems to keep the internal clock's period close to that of Earth's rotation. ■Yet despite this synchronization of the period of the internal cycle, the animal's timer itself continues to have its own genetically built-in period close to, but different from, 24 hours. ■Without the external cue, the difference accumulates and so the internally regulated activities of the biological day drift continuously, like the tides, in relation to the solar day. ■This drift has been studied extensively in many animals and in biological activities ranging from the hatching of fruit fly eggs to wheel running by squirrels. Light has a predominating influence in setting the clock. Even a fifteen-minute burst of light in otherwise sustained darkness can reset an animal's circadian rhythm. Normally, internal rhythms are kept in step by regular environmental cycles. For instance, if a homing pigeon is to navigate with its Sun compass, its clock must be properly set by cues provided by the daylight/darkness cycle.

4. Basic rules for good essays: Well-organized structure

4.1 Questions:

1) What is the thesis proposed by the author?
2) How are the paragraphs related to each other?
3) In what way does the author argues for the thesis?

4.2 Analysis:

This essay is well-organized with a clear structure that allows the author's exposition and argumentation to flow with ease.

Part One (Paragraph 1—4):

A detailed exposition of the close relationship between friendship and companionship by analyzing how those two kinds of relationship differ from and depend upon each other.

Paragraph 1 points out that friendship arise from companionship. A example about ancient hunters or warriors are referred to as evidence that friendship comes into being when companions are on the same route for the same goal.

Paragraph 2 asserts that unlike lovers, friends do not seek for privacy as much. (Pay attention here, this paragraph seems irrelevant in this position. The reason is that this is a selected part and this paragraph continues with the issues discussed previously which is not selected in Text 1.)

Paragraph 3 carries on the discussion in paragraph 1 by using examples of more contemporary settings.

Paragraph 4 identifies the subtle difference between friendship and companionship.

Paragraph 5 provides a deduction based on the analysis made before, that is, a possible explanation of some people's friendlessness.

Part Two (Paragraph 6—8):

A further introduction of the relationship between friendship and erotic love, namely, how the first evolves into the latter and how the latter influences the first.

Paragraph 6 indicates how friendship, which is originated from companionship between different sexes can transform into erotic love and also how erotic love also leads to friendship between the lovers.

Paragraph 7 provides an insight for modern people to realize the significance of the concept that friendship and erotic love exist at the same time.

Paragraph 8 is a complementary section to the previous paragraph.

Part Three (Paragraph 9—11):

The comment or the reflection of the previously-made assertion about the relationship between friendship and companionship.

Paragraph 9 brings forth people's common sense that friendship, which comes from companionship, is beneficial.

Paragraph 10 puts forward a possible controversy of the claim in paragraph 7 by doubting the "survival value" of friendship.

Paragraph 11 responses to such controversy by approaching the notion of "ally".

4.3 Working out an outline:

Please work out an outline on the topic "Can two people become friends if one person has more money than the other?" You may resort to the "Writing Process" in the Introduction of this book. Your writing plan should address at least the following questions:

1) How many parts and paragraphs do you plan to write?

2) What is the main idea for each paragraph?

3) What kind of examples will you use to illustrate the typical features of these two types of people?

II. Specific Writing Techniques

1. Defamiliarization

Defamiliarization is the artistic technique of forcing the audience to see common things in an unfamiliar way, in order to enhance perception of the familiar. The term "defamiliarization" was first coined in 1917 by Viktor Shklovsky, who invented the term as a means to distinguish poetic from practical language on the basis of the former's perceptibility. For a long time, poetic language is believed as being fundamentally different from ordinary speech. The author adopts such a technique in this text to formulate an extremely serious tone in approach such metaphysical and idealist concepts as friendship, companionship and erotic love. Please study the language in the following sentence:

It is when two such persons discover one another, when, whether with immense difficulties and semi-articulate fumblings or with what would seem to us amazing and elliptical speed, they share their vision it is then that Friendship is born.

Analysis: This sentence can be put into simple language like this: "If two persons, after long time of searching difficultly or easily, find that they share much in common, they can become friends." But such an expression is way too plain and simple. Through defamiliarization the words and expressions used by the author, such as "fumbling", "elliptical" and the sentence pattern such as "…what seem to us…" give rise to a unfamiliar and philosophical tone, which is apt for describing the essence of some abstract events and processes.

2. Figures of speech

In paragraph 10, some figures of speech are used. Please find them out and discuss them with your partners.

There is something in this. But nearly every reader would probably think some of these movements good for society and some bad. The whole list, if accepted, would tend to show, at best, that Friendship is both a possible benefactor and a possible danger to the community. And even as a benefactor it would have, not so much survival value, as what we may call "civilisation value"; would be something (in Aristotelian phrase) which helps the community not to live but to live well. Survival value and civilisation value coincide at some periods and in some circumstances, but not in all. What at any rate seems certain is that when Friendship bears fruit which the community can use it has to do so accidentally, as a byproduct. Religions devised for a social purpose, like Roman emperor-worship or modern attempts to sell Christianity as a means of "saving civilisation", do not come to much. The little knots of Friends who turn their backs on the "World" are those who really transform it. Egyptian and Babylonian Mathematics were practical and social, pursued in the service of Agriculture and Magic. But the free Greek Mathematics, pursued by Friends as a leisure occupation, have mattered to us more.

—Personification:

…Friendship is both a possible benefactor and a possible danger to the community.

The little knots of Friends who turn their backs on the "World" are those who really transform it.

—Metaphor:

What at any rate seems certain is that when Friendship <u>bears fruit</u> which the community can use it has to do so accidentally, as a <u>byproduct</u>.

The little <u>knots</u> of Friends who <u>turn their backs on</u> the "World" are those who really transform it.

3. Writing exercise:

Please paraphrase the following sentences into ordinary language and try to compare it with the original one. Find out what literary effects can be achieved.

1) Either you two will cease to be lovers but remain forever joint seekers of the same God, the same beauty, the same truth, or else, losing all that, you will retain as long as you live the raptures and ardours, all the wonder and the wild desire of Eros.

_____
_____
_____
_____

2) And conversely, erotic love may lead to Friendship between the lovers. But this, so far from obliterating the distinction between the two loves, puts it in a clearer light.

_____
_____
_____

III. Your Turn to Write

Please write an essay on the topic "Can two people become friends if one person has more money than the other?" Please give an outline first, arrange your paragraphs and justify your arrangement by considering carefully the relationship and development among all the paragraphs. Develop the paragraphs by examples and pay attention to its unity, cohesion and coherence. Finally, if you may, use some figurative language to vivify your writing.

Pearls of Wisdom

1. Have no friends not equal to yourself. —Confucius

2. A Friend may well be reckoned the masterpiece of Nature. —Ralph Waldo Emerson

3. Associate yourself with men of good quality if you esteem your own reputation; for it's better to be alone than in bad company. —George Washington

4. Be slow to fall into friendship; but when thou art in, continue firm and constant. —Socrates

Text B

Warming up

1. Do you have any foreign friends? How do you feel about them?
2. Do you consider cultural differences as a significant factor in making friends?
3. What qualities, do you believe, are considered as valuable and indispensable for all the countries in the world?

On Friendship

By Margaret Mead and Rhoda Metranx

A Critical Reader (I)

1. Few Americans stay put for a lifetime. We move from town to city to suburb, from high school to college in different state, from a job in one region to a better job elsewhere, from the home where we raise our children to the home where we plan to live in retirement. With each move we are forever making new friends, who become part of our new life at that time.

1 What is the function of this paragraph? Can we omit this paragraph and start with Paragraph 2?

2. For many of us the summer is a special time for forming new friendships. Today millions of Americans vocation abroad, and they go not only to see new sights but also—in those places where they do not feel too strange with the hope of meeting new people. No one really expects a vacation trip to produce a close friend. But surely the beginning of a friendship is possible? Surely in every country people value friendship?

2 Why summer is a special time for forming new friends?

3. They do. The difficulty when strangers from two countries meet is not a lack of appreciation of friendship, but different expectations about what

3 What is the relationship between Paragraph 3

constitutes friendship and how it comes into being. In those European countries that Americans are most likely to visit, friendship is quite sharply distinguished from other, more casual relations, and is differently related to family life. For a Frenchman, a German or an Englishman friendship is usually more special and carries a heavier burden of commitment[1].

4. But as we use the word, "friend" can be applied to wide range of relationships—to someone one has known for a few weeks in a new place, to a close business associate, to a childhood playmate, to a man or woman, to a trusted confidant[2]. There are real differences among these relations for Americans—a friendship may be superficial, casual, situational or deep and enduring. But to a European, who sees only our surface behavior, the differences are not clear.

5. As they see it, people known and accepted temporarily, casually, flow in and out of Americans' homes with little ceremony and often with little personal commitment. They may be parents of the children's friends, house guests of neighbors, members of a committee, business associates from another town or even another country. Coming as a guest into an American home, the European visitor finds no visible landmarks[3]. The atmosphere is relaxed. Most people, old and young, are called by first names.

6. Who then is a friend?

7. Even simple translation from one language to another is difficult. "You see," a Frenchman explains, "if I were to say to you in France, 'This is my good friend,' that person would not as close to me as someone about whom I said only, 'This is my friend.' Anyone about whom I have to say more is really less."

8. In France, as in many European countries, friends generally are of the same sex, and friendship is seen as basically a relationship between men. Frenchwomen laugh at the idea that "women can't be friends," but they also admit sometimes that for women "it's a different thing." And many French people doubt the possibility of a friendship between a man and a woman. There is also the kind of relationship with in a group—men and women who have worked together for a long time, who may be very close, sharing great loyalty and warmth of feeling. They may call one another—copains—a word that in English becomes "friends" but has more the

and Paragraph 2?

[4] What does Paragraph 4 mainly talk about?

[5] How is Paragraph 5 developed?

[6] Why is Paragraph 7 set up as an independent paragraph?

[7] How do French treat friendship between different sexes?

feeling of "pals" or "buddies". In French eyes this is not friendship, although two members of such a group may well be friends.

9. For the French, friendship is a one-to-one relationship that demands a keen awareness of the other person's intellect, temperament[4] and particular interests. A friend is someone who draws out your own best qualities, with whom you sparkle and become more of whatever the friendship draws upon. Your political philosophy assures more depth, appreciation of a play becomes sharper, taste in food or wine is enhanced[5], enjoyment of a sport is intensified.

10. And French friendships are divided into categories. A man may play chess with a friend for thirty years without knowing his political opinion, or he may talk politics with him for as long a time without knowing about his personal life. Different friends fill different niches in each person's life. These friendships are not made part of family life. A friend is not expected to spend evenings being nice to children or courteous to a deaf grandmother. Three duties, also serious and required, are primarily for relatives. Men who are friends may meet in a cafe. Intellectual friends may meet in larger groups for evenings of conversation. Working people may meet at the little bistro where they drink and talk, far from the family. Marriage does not affect such friendships; wives do not have to be taken into account.

11. In the past in France, friendships of this kind seldom were open to any but intellectual women. Since most women's lives centered on their homes, their warmest relations with other women often went back to their girlhood. The special relationship of friendship is based on what the French value most—on the mind, on having the same of outlook, on vivid awareness of some chosen area of life.

12. In Germany, in contrast with France, friendship is much more clearly a matter of feeling, adolescents, boys and girls, from deeply sentimental attachments, walk and talk together—not so much to polish their wits as to share their hopes and fears and dreams to form a common front against the world of school and family and to join in a kind of mutual discovery of each other's and their own inner life. Within the family, the closet relationship over a lifetime is between brothers and sisters. Outside the family, men and women find in their

[8] Why friendship in French is referred to as "a one-to-one" relationship?

[9] How is friendship in France distinguished from kinship?

[10] Do you detect some biased view in this paragraph?

[11] What characterize German friendship?

closet friends of the same sex the devotion of a sister, the loyalty of a brother. Appropriately, in Germany friends usually are brought into the family. Children call their father's and their mother's friends "uncle" and "aunt". Between French friends, who have chosen each other for the similarity of their point of view, lively disagreement and sharpness of argument are the breath of life. But for Germans, whose friendships are based on common feelings, deep disagreement on any subject that matters to both is regarded as a tragedy. Like ties of kinship, ties of friendship are meant to be absolutely binding. Young Germans who come to the United States have great difficulty in establishing such friendships with Americans. We view friendship more tentatively, subject to changes in intensity as people move, change their jobs, marry, or discover new interests.

13. English friendships follow still a different pattern. Their basis is shared activity. Activities at different stages of life may be of very different kinds—discovering a common interest in school, serving together in the armed forces, taking part in foreign mission, staying in the same country house during a crisis. In the midst of the activity, whatever it may be, people fall into step—sometimes two men or two women, sometimes two couples, sometimes three people—and find that they walk or play a game or tell stories or serve on a committee with the same easy anticipation of what each will do day by day or in some critical situation. Americans who have made English friends comment that, even years later, "you can take up just where you left off." Meeting after a long interval, friends are like a couple who begin to dance again when the orchestra strikes up after a pause. English friendships are formed outside the family circle, but they are not, as in Germany, committed to the family circle, but they are not, as in German, committed to the family nor are they, as in France, separated from the family. And a break in an English friendship comes not necessarily as a result of misjudgment, where one friend seriously misjudges how the other will think or feel or act, so that suddenly they are out of step.

12 How is friendship in England similar to and different from that in France?

14. What, then, is friendship? Looking at these different styles, including our own, each of which is related to a whole way of life, are there common elements? There is recognition that friendships are

formed, in contrast with kinship, though freedom of choice. A friend is someone who chooses and is chosen. Related to this is the sense each friend gives the other of being a special individual, on whatever grounds this recognition is based. And between friends there is inevitably a kind of equality of give and take.[6] These similarities make the bridge between societies possible, and the American's characteristic openness to different styles of relationship makes it possible for him to find new friends abroad with who he feels at home.

Notes

1. **commitment** /kə'mitmənt/ *n.* something pledged, especially an engagement by contract involving financial obligation.
2. **confidant** /'kɔnfidænt/ *n.* one to whom secrets or private matters are disclosed.
3. **landmark** /'lænd,maːk/ *n.* an event marking an important stage of development or a turning point in history.
4. **temperament** /'tempərəmənt/ *n.* the distinguishing mental and physical characteristics of a human being according to medieval physiology, resulting from dominance of one of the four humors.
5. **enhance** /in'haːns/ *v.* to make greater, as in value, beauty, or reputation; augment.
6. **give and take** /giv ænd teik/ *n.* mutual concessions, shared benefits, and cooperation.

A Critical Reader (II)

1. Please summarize the features of the friendship in each of these three countries respectively in your own words, and think about which group of people you like to make friends with most.
2. Can you imitate the way that the author introduces these three different types of friendship and give a brief account of the friendship among Chinese? So far as you know, which is the most ideal friends type for Chinese, French, Germans or Englishmen?
3. According to the author, friendship can be vastly difference across cultures. Are those differences inherent or accidental? Can you dig this topic further and find out what lies behind all such superficial differences of the attitudes, insights, and inclinations toward friendship in those three countries?

A Critical Writer

I. Basic Writing Techniques

1. Style and word choice

1.1 This article deals with a highly complex topic: the comparison of friendship between different cultures. Since friendship itself is virtually an abstract and ambiguous term from an academic point of view, to handle it from a cross-cultural perspective adds more challenge and intricateness to the writing task. However, the author manages to tackle this problem by depicting such a profound issue in highly comprehensive and generalized language. In this way, the message that is contained in each sentence is conveyed efficiently and effectively. At the same time, this seemingly boring and metaphysical topic becomes more approachable for ordinary readers.

1.2 Please notice the words and expressions in the following sentences:

The difficulty when strangers from two countries meet is not <u>a lack of appreciation</u> of friendship, but different <u>expectations</u> about what constitutes friendship and how it <u>comes into being</u>. (Paragraph 3)

There are real differences among these relations for Americans—a friendship may be <u>superficial</u>, <u>casual</u>, <u>situational</u> or <u>deep and enduring</u>. (Paragraph 4)

As they see it, people known and accepted <u>temporarily</u>, <u>casually</u>, <u>flow in and</u> out of Americans' homes with little ceremony and often with little <u>personal commitment</u>. (Paragraph 5)

For the French, friendship is a <u>one-to-one relationship</u> that demands a <u>keen awareness of the other person's intellect, temperament and particular interests</u>. (Paragraph 9)

And French friendships are <u>divided into categories</u>. (Paragraph 10)

A friend is someone <u>who chooses and is chosen</u>. Related to this is the sense each friend gives the other of being a special individual, on whatever grounds this recognition is based. And between friends there is inevitably a kind of equality of <u>give and take</u>. (Paragraph 14)

2. Good structure in the level of paragraph and essay

2.1 Questions:

1) How many parts does the essay consist of? What are they?
2) How does each part connect with one another?
3) How are the points that the author intends to make arranged?
4) How is each paragraph developed?

2.2 Analysis:

1) This essay is structured in two parts.

Part One (Paragraphs 1—3) is the first part, serving as a lead-in section. In this part, the author justifies himself in writing this essay by pointing out the necessity for Americans of making new friends in a new place, both because Americans are rootless and full of wanderlust and because formation of a cross-cultural friendship is possible.

Part Two (Paragraphs 4—6) in a natural development of the thesis. Friendship in three typical countries, France, German and England are expounded and compared in a substantial way.

2) On the paragraph level, the author follows strictly some basic rules for paragraph development in a textbook manner. Paragraphs are developed by examples, by reasoning, by comparison and contrast and so on. The structure of a topic sentence, a controlling idea, a succession of supporting ideas and a conclusion can be identified clearly.

Paragraph 8

In France, as in many European countries, friends generally are of the same sex, and friendship is seen as basically a relationship between men. Frenchwomen laugh at the idea that "women can't be friends," but they also admit sometimes that for women "it's a different thing." And many French people doubt the possibility of a friendship between a man and a woman. There is also the kind of relationship with in a group—men and women who have worked together for a long time, who may be very close, sharing great loyalty and warmth of feeling. They may call one another—copains—a word that in English becomes "friends" but has more the feeling of "pals" or "buddies". In French eyes this is not friendship, although two members of such a group may well be friends. (Development by classification, cause and effect.)

Paragraph 10

And French friendships are divided into categories. A man may play chess with a friend for thirty years without knowing his political opinion, or he may talk politics with him for as long a time without knowing about his personal life. Different friends fill different niches in each person's life. These friendships are not made part of family life. A friend is not expected to spend evenings being nice to children or courteous to a deaf grandmother. Three duties, also serious and required, are primarily for relatives. Men who are friends may meet in a cafe. Intellectual friends may meet in larger groups for evenings of conversation. Working people may meet at the little bistro where they drink and talk, far from the family. Marriage does not affect wuch friendships; wives do not have to be taken into account. (Development by examples. Please pay attention to the "topic sentence plus supporting ideas pattern" .)

Please analyze the rest of paragraphs by yourself.

II. Your Turn to Write

China is a country famous for its respect for politeness and good manners. And in Confucianism, loyalty, honesty and kindness are regarded as valuable and decisive indicators for a gentleman. Influenced deeply by such philosophy, the Chinese friendship has its unique characteristics. Discuss these characteristics with your partner and write an essay entitled "On Chinese Friendship". You may imitate the way that the author of this text writes about friendship and makes comparisons among friendship of different cultures.

Pearls of Wisdom

1. Culture, the acquainting ourselves with the best that has been known and said in the world, and thus with the history of the human spirit.   —Matthew Arnold

2. Society is unity in diversity.   —George H. Mead

3. At bottom every man knows well enough that he is a unique being, only once on this earth; and by no extraordinary chance will such a marvelously picturesque piece of diversity in unity as he is, ever be put together a second time.   —Friedrich Nietzsche

Text C

For Immediate Release

By Paul Simms

A Critical Reader

1. Alex Kerner (C.E.O., C.O.O.[1], chairman, and president of Alex Kerner's Personal Life, Inc.) announced today a wide-ranging restructuring of his imaginary company's upper management.

2. Tim Williams, a member of the company in varying capacities for five years, has been promoted to Best Friend, and he will report directly to Kerner in all friendship-related matters.

3. "Tim has proved himself to be a solid guy who's always up for whatever," Kerner says. "During the past five years, I've watched him excel in every position he's occupied. From Mere Acquaintance to Periodic Dinner Companion (In Groups of Four or More People) to Frequent Midweek Business-Lunch Cohort, Tim has consistently shown himself to be just the kind of person we're looking for in a Best Friend.

4. "Tim's willingness to charge midweek lunches to his expense account represents just one element in a strategic alliance[2] that will be an asset for both of us far into the future."

5. The former holder of the Best Friend position, Lou Solomon, will not be leaving the organization but, rather, will be transitioning into the newly created post of Independent Phone Acquaintance.

1 What is the genre of this writing according to the first paragraph?

2 What do we know about Tim?

3 What happens to Lou?

6. "As my Best Friend for the past few years, Lou has shepherded our outfit through more than a few successful endeavors," Kerner says. "He was our point man on the Night I Puked in a Cab. He was a sage adviser on the Night I Lost One Shoe. And he was indispensable[3] in quickly assembling a crisis-response team on the Night I Lost My Phone but Then We Found It in His Futon.

7. "Lou also pioneered the 'poison pill' defense, whereby we pretended to be Mutual Friends with Tom Monroe, a known dick, thus staving off a hostile-takeover attempt by Jack Houlihan & Friends, L.L.C."

8. "Drinking and Puking and Losing Things will always be a core part of our business," Kerner says. "But, as we focus on diversifying into Non-Drinking and Puking and Losing Things-related areas, we feel that Lou's skills can be put to better use elsewhere. Regardless, I look forward to speaking to Lou every once in a while on the phone if I'm not too busy for many years to come."

9. Also affected in the restructuring is Solomon's girlfriend, Kay Madison, who was increasingly involved in all of Kerner and Solomon's activities, despite the fact that she technically reported solely to Solomon.

10. "I wish Kay all the best in her future endeavors," Kerner says. "I know she was often frustrated by her lack of direct access to me—except through Lou—but I doubt that she'll be without a solid friendship position for long, as there are many organizations out there looking for a bold, brassy, loud, and opinionated[4] woman who is hell-bent on finding a way to insert herself into every aspect of the friendship structure."

11. In a reshuffling move unrelated to the current streamlining, former Best Platonic Female Friend Lisa Mayberry has been summarily terminated from the organization for malfeasance involving telling Kerner's ex-girlfriend details about Kerner's current girlfriend.

12. "We hold all our employees—from Best Friend for Life, Emeritus, on down to 'Hey, How You Doing, We Don't Know Each Other's Names, but We Live in the Same Building'-level Elevator Companions—to a strict standard of conduct," Kerner says. "And there's simply no room in this organization for a yappy gossip who I suspect was always just waiting for me to be between

[4] What kind of friendship do they hold?

[5] What role does Kay play in their friendship? Do they like Kay, why?

[6] What does the first sentence mean?

girlfriends and depressed so she could try to trick me into sleeping with her."

13. Kerner is also exploring a possible merger with a onetime competitor, the Bill Schofield Group. Schofield's assets include fairly good Knicks season tickets and at least one semi-famous friend.

14. "We're not looking to steal Bill's old college buddy Dan Abrams from him," Kerner says. "But, if we could become friends with him as part of the bargain[5], that would represent a win-win for all involved."

15. Also, Ahmed Humza—a seven-year veteran in the Friendly but Nameless Newsstand Operator post—has been promoted to the newly created position of Ahmed.

16. "I've been going to that same newsstand every day for seven years," Kerner says. "I don't know why, but recently I finally asked the guy what his name is. Though I doubt Ahmed will ever rise to the 'You're Allowed in My Apartment' level of upper management, he will serve as a significant rhetorical asset to be used in arguments about terrorism when the other person says, 'O.K., but I bet you don't even have any Arab friends.'"

17. Finally, despite rumors to the contrary, Kerner has reaffirmed that Tom Monroe will continue to fill the post of That Dick.

18. "I found myself standing next to Tom at a party recently, and we had a cordial conversation," Kerner says. "But anyone who says that we're Friends—or even Mutual Tolerators—is sorely mistaken. I want nothing to do with that dick."

7 What kind of person is Ahmed Humza?

Notes

1. **C. O. O.** short for Chief Operation Officer
2. **alliance** /əˈlaɪəns/ *n.* a close association of nations or other groups, formed to advance common interests or causes.
3. **indispensable** /ˌɪndɪˈspensəb(ə)l/ *adj.* not to be dispensed with; essential..
4. **opinionated** /əˈpɪnjəneɪtɪd/ *adj.* holding stubbornly and often unreasonably to one's own opinions.
5. **bargain** /ˈbɑːɡɪn/ *n.* an agreement establishing the terms of a sale or exchange of goods or services.

A Critical Writer

I. Questions for Discussion

1. What is the unique style adopted in this writing? What does this article talk about? Why does the author choose to write this article in this way?

2. In this article, large amount of terms and expressions of news reports are borrowed. Please find them out and write a real news report of your own.

3. Pick up the words and expressions you like best and share them with your partners.

II. Your Turn to Write

Based on the analysis made above, For Immediate Release is written in a form of press release, which is a relatively rare form for writing about something other than news events. Usually, abstract topics, like friendship, are written of an argumentative or expositional style. Such a "foregrounding" creates a special literary effect that greatly amuses its readers. Can you follow this foregrounding strategy and write a story of you and your friends with a style that is not generally adopted for writing a story? For example, the writing style of a drug instruction or machine manual book? Have a try.

Pearls of Wisdom

1. "Anybody can sympathise with the sufferings of a friend, but it requires a very fine nature to sympathise with a friend's success." —Oscar Wilde

2. "Those friends thou hast, and their adoption tried,
   Grapple them to thy soul with hoops of steel;
   But do not dull thy palm with entertainment
   Of each new-hatch'd, unfledg'd comrade."
   — William Shakespeare

3. "What sunshine is to flowers, smiles are to humanity. They are but trifles, to be sure but, scattered along life's pathway, the good they do is inconceivable." —Anonymous

4. "No soul is desolate as long as there is a human being for whom it can feel trust and reverence." —George Eliot

Corpus-based Exercises (4)

I. Key Word: activity

1. The essence of friendship is the theme of both Text A and Text B, in which many friendship-related activities are mentioned. Actually the word *activity* is used by the authors several times.

- For us of course, the **shared activity** and therefore the companionship on which Friendship supervenes will not often be a bodily one like hunting or fighting.
- English friendships follow still a different pattern. Their basis is **shared activity**. Activities at different stages of life may be of very different kinds.

The following are some concordance lines of activity from a corpus:

n education , we place no value on intellectual	activity	. We Americans are a charitable and
g ? To begin with , it is purposeful mental	activity	over which we exercise some contro
rowing population and intensifying economic	activity	are increasingly destroying forests a
ways to ease the tension . / Try physical	activity	. When you 're nervous , angry or up
ey come from . / The result of all this	activity	is clubs have to shop at the global su 5
tal money is traceable and can hinder illegal	activity	of all kinds . Other important benefit
n and enterprise across the broadest range of	activity	. In the national Teaching Quality A
, no one yet knows how much damage human	activity	is doing to the environment . Human
ows second-by-second observation of brain	activity	. At several American universities ,
which kind of trial they were in . / Brain	activity	in certain neural systems seemed to 10
n't eat meat and have a high level of physical	activity	. " (An estimated 15 percent of mal
fic studies of animals implies that physical	activity	has a positive effect on mental funct
rats have demonstrated two primary effects of	activity	: vigorous physical exercise provide
e ability and the gifted girls showed strong	activity	on both sides of their brains as they t
d very differently . There was a sudden drop in	activity	in the left side of the brain — the sid 15
eek period during our teenage years , chemical	activity	in the brain is cut in half . That done
nival , a religious ritual , or some economic	activity	. Yet the visitor should never forget
and they vastly misrepresent competitive	activity	within private- property markets . In
d aggression can be expressed in constructive	activity	and non-violent competition , will th
ere killed or harmed as the result of a particular	activity	over a certain period of time ; the de 20
tells us how many people were involved in that	activity	during that time . All risk levels are t
s , the closer it is to 1 , the riskier the	activity	in question . In the case just discusse
themselves to read . Teaching is also public	activity	: It can be seen and observed . / L
described as dropping or quitting of an	activity	that was at one time enjoyable . The

2. Please try to remember the following collocations and expressions of activity drawn from the above concordance lines.

group activity	electrical activity
mental activity	chemical activity
intellectual activity	economic activity
sports activity	illegal activity
shared activity	natural activity
mental activity	suspicious activity
physical activity	free activity
recreational activities	civic activity

3. Please translate the following Chinese sentences into English using collocations and expressions of activity you have learned from Text B and the above concordance lines.

1) 这个实验的主要目的是检验实验对象在睡眠中的大脑活动。

_____

2) 他们同是动漫社的成员，共同的兴趣、爱好共同参与的活动为他们的友谊打下基础。

_____

3) 此次行动旨在打击火车站周边的不法行为。

_____

4) 多多参与集体活动有益于抑郁症的治疗。

_____

5) 第一眼见到她，他就爱上了她。

_____

6) 当地的经济发展为政府带来了丰厚的收入，同时也对环境造成了严重破坏。

_____

II. Key Word: relationship

1. *Friendship* is in essence a kind of human relationship. It is also necessary for us to understand in depth the collocation of the word "relationship".

ance will be woven through a loving	**relationship**	, and reviving it now and then is
ss , some degree of romance in a new	**relationship**	. That 's part of what makes a rel
eal affection and enrich an ongoing	**relationship**	. It 's sincere . It pleases both par
y for an intense one-to-one emotional	**relationship**	with an older person . The child
eve and I had a fluctuating	**relationship**	. A separation of five years in ag
civilization being created is a new	**relationship**	between development and under
world , the general character of the	**relationship**	is cooperation and construction ,
ord , " love " to describe an intimate	**relationship**	with a boyfriend or girlfriend , t

5

d devoted to one another . The loving	relationship	between my parents and me is st
and , but it is also a give-and-take	relationship	. In my experience , loving frien
s to maintain a strong and rewarding	relationship	. But the payoff , the love that th
isolates indicates that a causal	relationship	exists between groundward trop
power of the media , our love-hate	relationship	with technology . / " I remem
n that I began to think a lot about the	relationship	between fathers and sons and to
efore marriage and has only a casual	relationship	with the father , or she might ha
There is a natural tendency for any	relationship	based on voluntary affection to c
ortunately , has replaced a permanent	relationship	with a new ideal of unlimited ch
marriage exists only as a romantic	relationship	that can be ended at will , and fa
large sample of studies , no overall	relationship	between grades and adult achiev
rge sample of studies , no overall	relationship	between grades and adult achiev
only	relationship	that needs forgiveness . It 's requ
en strangers . In fact , no human	relationship	can survive without the oxygen
riendship is a one-to-one	relationship	that demands a keen awareness
nt back to their girlhood . The special	relationship	of friendship is based on what th
fe . Within the family , the closet	relationship	over a lifetime is between broth
teristic openness to different styles of	relationship	makes it possible for him to find
nternet . The process of an online	relationship	; however , is very dat
ved in online romances describe their	relationship	in these terms : " I 'en

(Line numbers: 10, 15, 20, 25)

2. Please try to remember the following collocations and expressions of *relationship* drawn from the above concordance lines.

casual relationship	be woven through a relationship
emotional relationship	create relationship
human relationship	describe a relationship
intimate relationship	enrich an ongoing relationship
love-hate relationship	have a fluctuating relationship
loving relationship	indicate relationship
ongoing relationship	maintain relationship
online relationship	
permanent relationship	
romantic relationship	
special relationship	
strong and rewarding relationship	

3. Please translate the following Chinese sentence into English, trying to use the collocations and expressions from the above concordance lines.

1) 心理医生分析后认为，他的暴行与童年时的严重创伤有关。

2) 专家认为教师在课外应与学生保持一定距离，避免过于亲密的师生关系。

3) 朋友间的彼此信任和忠诚是加深友谊的基石。

4) 网络上的人际关系通常肤浅且不稳定，也是某些犯罪行为的源头。

5) 自从上周的争执以后，他与上层的关系开始变得不稳定。

6) 对于任何一家公司来说，最困难的业务往往不是建立新客户，而是维持与老客户的关系。

Education

Warming up

1. Education is one of the building blocks for the development of individuals and human beings as a whole. Please discuss the significance and purpose of education with your partners.
2. Are you satisfied with the current education system in China? What are the most satisfying and unsatisfying parts in your own personal education experience? Suppose you are Minister of Education, what are you going to do to put your ideals of education into practice?

Text A

The great educational theorist's most concise statement of his ideas about the needs, the problems, and the possibilities of education—written after his experience with the progressive schools and in the light of the criticisms his theories received.

Experience and Education (selected)

By John Dewey

A Critical Reader

1. MANKIND likes to think in terms of extreme opposites. It is given to formulating its beliefs in terms of Either-Or, between which it recognizes no intermediate possibilities. When forced to recognize that the extremes cannot be acted upon, it is still inclined to hold that they are all right in theory but that when it comes to practical matters circumstances compel us to compromise. Educational philosophy is no exception. The history of educational theory is marked by opposition between the idea that education is development from within and that it is formation from without; that it is based upon natural endowments and that education is a process of overcoming natural inclination[1] and substituting in its place habits acquired under external pressure.

1 What does "extreme opposite mean?" Can you give other examples of someone who "thinks in terms of extreme opposite" in your daily life? Why does the author mention it at the very beginning of this article?

2. <u>At present, the opposition, so far as practical affairs of the school are concerned, tends to take the form of contrast between traditional and progressive education.</u> If the underlying ideas of the former are formulated broadly, without the qualification required for accurate statement, they are found to be about as follows: The subject-matter of education consists of bodies of information and of skills that have been worked out in the past; therefore, the chief business of the school is to transmit them to the new generation. In the past, there have also been developed standards and rules of conduct; moral training consists in forming habits of action in conformity with these rules and standards. Finally, the general pattern of school organization (by which I mean the relations of pupils to one another and to the teachers) constitutes the school kind of institution sharply marked off from other social institutions. Call up in imagination the ordinary school-room, its time schedules, schemes of classification, of examination and promotion, of rules of order, and I think you will grasp what is meant by "pattern of organization." If then you contrast this scene with what goes on in the family, for example, you will appreciate what is meant by the school being a kind of institution sharply marked off from any other form of social organization.

3. The three characteristics just mentioned fix the aims and methods of instruction and discipline. The main purpose or objective is to prepare the young for future responsibilities and for success in life, by means of acquisition of the organized bodies of information and prepared forms of skill, which comprehend the material of instruction. Since the subject matter as well as standards of proper conduct pre handed down from the part, the attitude of pupils must, upon the whole, be one of docility, receptivity and obedience. Books, especially textbooks, are the chief representatives of the lore and wisdom of the past, while teachers are the organs through which pupils rue brought into effective connection with the material. Teachers are the agents through which knowledge and skills are communicated and rules of conduct enforced.

4. I have not made this brief summary for the purpose of criticizing the underlying philosophy. The rise of what is called new education and progressive schools is of itself a product of discontent with

2 What is the structural function of this sentence?

3 Please summarize the three characteristics of traditional education in your own words.

4 How are the ideas in the previous paragraph developed in this paragraph?

traditional education. In effect it is the criticism of the latter. When the implied criticism is made explicit it reads somewhat as follows: The traditional scheme is, in essence, one of imposition from above and from outside. It imposes adult standards, subject-matter, and methods upon those who are only growing slowly toward maturity. The gap is so great that the required subject matter, the methods of learning and of behaving are foreign to the existing capacities of the young. They are beyond the reach of the experience the young learners already possess. Consequently, they must be imposed; even though good teachers will use devices of art to cover up the imposition[2] so as to relieve it of obviously brutal features.

5. But the gulf between the mature or adult products and the experience and abilities of the young is so wide that the very situation forbids much active participation by pupils in the development of what is taught. Theirs is to do—and learn, as it was the part of the six hundred to do and die. Learning here means acquisition[3] of what already is incorporated in books and in the heads of the elders. Moreover, that which is taught is thought of as essentially static. It is taught as a finished product, with little regard either to the ways in which it was originally built up or to changes that will surely occur in the future. It is to a large extent the cultural product of societies that assumed the future would be much like the past, and yet it is used as educational food in a society where change is the rule, not the exception. If one attempts to formulate the philosophy of education implicit in the practices of the new education, we may, I think, discover certain common principles amid the variety of progressive schools now existing. To imposition from above is opposed expression and cultivation of individuality; to external discipline is opposed free activity; to learning from texts and teachers, learning through experience; to acquisition of isolated skills and techniques by drill, is opposed acquisition of them as means of attaining ends which make direct vital appeal; to preparation for a more or less remote future is opposed making the most of the opportunities of present life; to static aims and materials is opposed acquaintance[4] with a changing world.

6. Now, all principles by themselves are abstract. They become concrete only in the consequences, which result from their application. Just because the

5 According to the author, what is the greatest problem of traditional education?

6 How many points does the author make to criticize the "imposition" manner in traditional education?

7 How is the "new education" different from the traditional education?

principles set forth are so fundamental and far-reaching[5], everything depends upon the interpretation given them as they are put into practice in the school and the home. It is at this point that the reference made earlier to Either-Or philosophies becomes peculiarly pertinent. The general philosophy of the new education may be sound, and yet the difference in abstract principles will not decide the way in which the moral and intellectual preference involved shall be worked out in practice. There is always the danger in a new movement that in rejecting the aims and methods of that which it would supplant, it may develop its principles negatively rather than positively and constructively. Then it takes its clew in practice from that which is rejected instead of from the constructive development of its own philosophy.

7. I take it that the fundamental unity of the newer philosophy is found in the idea that there is an intimate and necessary relation between the processes of actual experience and education. If this be true, then a positive and constructive development of its own basic idea depends upon having a correct idea of experience. Take, for example, the question of organized subject-matter—which will be discussed in some detail later. The problem for progressive education is: What is the place and meaning of subject-matter and of organization within experience? How does subject-matter function? Is there anything inherent in experience, which tends towards progressive organization of its contents? What results follow when the materials of experience are not progressively organized? A philosophy which proceeds on the basis of rejection, of sheer opposition, will neglect these questions. It will tend to suppose that because the old education was based on ready-made organization, therefore it successes to reject the principle of organization into to, instead of striving to discover what it means and how it is to be attained on the basis of experience. We might go through all the points of difference between the new and the old education and reach similar conclusions. When external control is rejected, the problem becomes that of finding the factors of control that are inherent within experience. When external authority is rejected, it does not follow that all authority should be rejected, but rather that there is need to search for a more effective source of authority. Because the older education imposed the knowledge,

[8] What is the main idea of this paragraph? Why does the author put this paragraph in this place?

[9] What are the similar conclusions that both the

methods, and the rules of conduct of the mature person upon the young, it does not follow, except upon the basis of the extreme Either-Or philosophy, that the knowledge and skill of the mature person has no directive value for the experience of the immature. On the contrary, basing education upon personal experience may mean more multiplied and more intimate contacts between the mature and the immature than ever existed in the traditional school, and consequently more, rather than less, guidance by others. The problem, then, is: how these contacts can be established without violating the principle of learning through personal experience. The solution of this problem requires a well thought-out philosophy of the social factors that operate in the constitution of individual experience.

8. What is indicated in the foregoing remarks is that the general principles of the new education do not of themselves solve any of the problems of the actual or practical conduct and management of progressive schools. Rather, they set new problems which have to be worked out on the basis of a new philosophy of experience. The problems are not even recognized, to say nothing of being solved, when it is assumed that it suffices to reject the ideas and practices of the old education and then go to the opposite extreme. Yet I am sure that you will appreciate what is meant when I say that many of the newer schools tend to make little or nothing of organized subject-matter of study; to proceed as if any form of direction and guidance by adults were an invasion of individual freedom, and as if the idea that education should be concerned with the present and future meant that acquaintance with the past has little or no role to play in education. Without pressing these defects to the point of exaggeration, they at least illustrate what is meant by a theory and practice of education which proceeds negatively or by reaction against what has been current in education rather than by a positive and constructive development of purposes, methods, and subject-matter on the foundation of a theory of experience and its educational potentialities.

9. It is not too much to say that an educational philosophy which professes to be based on the idea of freedom may become as dogmatic as ever was the traditional education which is reacted against. For any theory and set of practices is dogmatic which is not

old and new education might reach? What's the point the author tries to make here?

10 How is the first paragraph reflected in this paragraph?

11 In this paragraph, the author admits that mistaken deeds are practiced in some progressive schools, what are they?

based upon critical examination of its own underlying principles. Let us say that the new education emphasizes the freedom of the learner. Very well. A problem is now set. What does freedom mean and what are the conditions under which it is capable of realization? Let us say that the kind of eternal imposition which was so common in the traditional school limited rather than promoted the intellectual and moral development of the young. Again, very well. Recognition of this serious defect sets a problem. Just what is the role of the teacher and of books in promoting the educational development of the immature Admit that traditional education employed as the subject-matter for study facts and ideas so bound up with the past as to give little help in dealing with the issues of the present and future. Very well. Now we have the problem of discovering the connection which actually exists within experience between the achievements of the past and the issues of the present. We have the problem of ascertaining[6] how acquaintance with the past may be translated into a potent instrumentality for dealing effectively with the future. We may reject knowledge of the past as the end of education and thereby only emphasize its importance as a means. When we do that we have a problem that is new in the story of education: How shall the young become acquainted with the past in such a way that the acquaintance is a potent agent in appreciation of the living present?

12 How is this article ended by this paragraph?

Notes

1. inclination /ˌɪnkləˈneɪʃən/ n.   a characteristic disposition to do, prefer, or favor one thing rather than another; a propensity
2. imposition /ˌɪmpəˈzɪʃən/ n.   the act of imposing or the condition of being imposed
3. acquisition /ˌækwɪˈzɪʃən/ n.   to gain possession of
4. acquaintance /əˈkweɪntəns/ n.   knowledge of a person acquired by a relationship less intimate than friendship
5. far-reaching /ˈfɑːˈriːtʃɪŋ/ adj.   having a wide range, influence, or effect
6. ascertain /ˌæsəˈteɪn/ v.   to discover with certainty, as through examination or experimentation

A Critical Reader (II)

1 Do you agree with Dewey's philosophy that education should be based on experience rather that the imposition of knowledge? Experience and books, which is a better source of knowledge?

2 Try to compare the problems you listed of Chinese education system in the warming up section with the ones that Dewey addresses in this article about traditional education. Discuss with your partners again about what you find out after the comparison.

A Critical Writer

I. Basic Writing Techniques

1. Style and word choice

Experience and Education is the best concise statement on education ever published by John Dewey, who is acknowledged to be the pre-eminent educational theorist of the twentieth century. Written more than two decades after *Democracy and Education* (Dewey's most comprehensive statement of his position in educational philosophy), this book demonstrates how Dewey reformulated his ideas as a result of his intervening experience with the progressive schools and in the light of the criticisms his theories had received.

The selected part is the first chapter of this book. The author adopted a writing style that is consistent with the incoming parts in terms of choice of vocabulary, order of words within a sentence and even punctuation. Generally speaking, a _____ (A. scholastic   B. funny   C. ironical) and authentic tone is adopted which allows the points of in this article to be developed in a/n _____ (A. sensitive   B. emotional   C. objective) and persuasive way.

As for the level of diction, the author tends to use a (A. casual   B. standard   C. formal) vocabulary all the way through, since this particular writing is for _____(A. common   B. highly educated   C. local) readers and scholars. Therefore, the diction gives every appearance of intellectuality and authenticity. Please pay attention to the highlighted words and expressions.

1) The main purpose or **objective** is to prepare the young for future responsibilities and for success in life, **by means of acquisition** of the organized **bodies of information** and prepared forms of skill, which **comprehend the material of instruction**. (Paragraph 3).

2) The gap is so great that the required subject matter, the methods of learning and of behaving **are foreign to** the existing capacities of the young. (Paragraph 4)

3) Just because the principles set forth are so **fundamental and far-reaching**, everything depends upon the **interpretation** given them as they are put into practice in the school and the home. (Paragraph 6)

4) It is at this point that the reference made earlier to Either-Or philosophies becomes **peculiarly pertinent**. (Paragraph 6)

5) It is not too much to say that an educational philosophy which **professes** to be based on the idea of freedom may become **as dogmatic** as ever was the traditional education **which is reacted against**. (Paragraph 9)

Please find out more of such examples by yourself.

2. Basic rules for good sentences

2.1 Unity: one single, complete thought.

Please read the following two sentences and try to find out how unity is displayed:

1) Since the subject matter as well as standards of proper conduct pre handed down from the part, the attitude of pupils must, upon the whole, be one of docility, receptivity and obedience. (Paragraph 3)

2) There is always the danger in a new movement that in rejecting the aims and methods of that which it would supplant, it may develop its principles negatively rather than positively and constructively. (Paragraph 6)

Please find out more of such examples by yourself.

2.2 Coherence: clear connection between parts; no faulty parallel constructions, no unknown pronouns, no unclear relationships.

Please read the following sentence and try to find out how coherence is displayed:

When external authority is rejected, it does not follow that all authority should be rejected, but rather that there is need to search for a more effective source of authority. (Paragraph 7)

Please find out more of such examples by yourself.

2.3 Conciseness: no unnecessary words.

Please convey the meaning of the following sentence in English:

传统教育从很大程度来讲是社会的文化产物，其总是假设社会的未来发展会遵循过去既成的发展轨迹，从而把过往的社会发展经验又作为教育的内容教授给学生。而这一作法忽略了这样一个事实：社会在不断发展变化，并非一成不变。

_____

_____

_____

_____

Now please compare what you write with the text and find out how conciseness is achieved:

It is to a large extent the cultural product of societies that assumed the future would be much like the past, and yet it is used as educational food in a society where change is the rule, not the exception. (Paragraph 5)

Please find out more of such examples by yourself.

2.4 Good grammar: good structure, good use of articles (a, an, the), accurate spelling,

and clear punctuation.

Please analyze the structure, the use of articles, and the punctuation of the following sentence.

Yet I am sure that you will appreciate what is meant when I say that many of the newer schools tend to make little or nothing of organized subject-matter of study; to proceed as if any form of direction and guidance by adults were an invasion of individual freedom, and as if the idea that education should be concerned with the present and future meant that acquaintance with the past has little or no role to play in education.(Paragraph 8)

3. Basic rules for good paragraphs

3.1 Please read Paragraph 1 again and do the following exercises:

1) **Unity**: a central theme; clear topic sentence, and all sentences with the paragraph relate to the topic sentence.

2) **Coherence**: proper order; each sentence leads smoothly and logical to the next sentence.

3) **Development**: the paragraph has sufficient information to support the topic sentence.

4) **Good transition**: use of transition words that move the reader between thoughts and paragraphs.

Please find out how unity and coherence are displayed:

MANKIND likes to think in terms of extreme opposites. It is given to formulating its beliefs in terms of Either-Or, between which it recognizes no intermediate possibilities. When forced to recognize that the extremes cannot be acted upon, it is still inclined to hold that they are all right in theory but that when it comes to practical matters circumstances compel us to compromise. Educational philosophy is no exception. The history of educational theory is marked by opposition between the idea that education is development from within and that it is formation from without; that it is based upon natural endowments and that education is a process of overcoming natural inclination and substituting in its place habits acquired under external pressure.(Paragraph 1)

3.2 Analysis:

1) **Unity**: this paragraph displays good unity.

The first sentence is the topic sentence of the whole paragraph with the controlling idea "extreme opposites" and this controlling idea is reflected in almost every sentence that follows:

Sentence 2: It is given to formulating its beliefs in terms of <u>Either-Or</u>, between which it recognizes <u>no intermediate possibilities</u>.

Sentence 3: When forced to recognize that <u>the extremes</u> cannot be acted upon, it is still inclined to hold that they are all right in theory but that when it comes to practical matters circumstances compel us to compromise.

Sentence 5: The history of educational theory is marked by <u>opposition between the idea</u> that education is development from within <u>and</u> that it is formation from without; that it is based upon natural endowments <u>and</u> that education is a process of overcoming natural inclination and substituting in its place habits acquired under external pressure.

Please pay attention: sentence 5 is a more detailed explanation of the controlling idea "extreme opposites". Since the "extreme opposites" refers to something containing two sides, the two "and" (highlighted) are symbols that "extreme opposites" are explained, since there is something in front of the "and" and something after the "and", the term "extreme opposites" are reflected and explained in detail.

2) **Coherence**: This paragraph displays good coherence.

Please notice the relation of each sentence:

Sentence 1: MANKIND likes to think in terms of extreme opposites.

Sentence 2: It is given to formulating its beliefs in terms of Either-Or, between which it recognizes no intermediate possibilities.

Analysis: In this sentence, the "It" at the very beginning refers to the subjective of the previous sentence, "MANKIND". The expressions "Either-Or" and "no intermediate possibilities" refer to the concept of "extreme opposites" in the previous sentence as well. In this way, the two sentences are connected and coherent.

Sentence 3: When forced to recognize that the extremes cannot be acted upon, it is still inclined to hold that they are all right in theory but that when it comes to practical matters circumstances compel us to compromise.

Analysis: This sentence is a continual and natural development of the previous sentence. Pay attention to the word "still".

Sentence 4: Educational philosophy is no exception (of such thinking pattern of MANKIND)

Analysis: This sentence serves as a logical summary of the previous three sentences, which also transits the paragraph to the next point, i.e. the application of general human thinking pattern to education. Please note that the omitted information (in the bracket) is implied, rather than explicitly written.

Sentence 5: The history of educational theory is marked by opposition between the idea that education is development from within and that it is formation from without; that it is based upon natural endowments and that education is a process of overcoming natural inclination and substituting in its place habits acquired under external pressure.

Analysis: This sentence is a follow-up of sentence 4, explaining and developing the core concept of educational philosophy. Please pay attention, the subjectives of both sentences include the word "education."

3) **Development**: This paragraph displays good development.

As we have discussed above, each sentence develops its previous sentence with more detailed explanation (as is exemplified by sentence 1, sentence 2 and sentence 3). This is also called progression.

4) **Transition**:

Sentence 4 serves as a transitional sentence in this paragraph, which turns the point of this paragraph from the general philosophy to the educational philosophy.

3.3 Imitation:

Please try to write a paragraph starting by the given topic sentence. You may imitate paragraph 1 to achieve its unity, coherence and development.

1) Women tend to be more sensitive than men. _____
_____
_____
_____
_____

2) Compared with living off the campus, living on campus is a preferable choice for most students _____
_____
_____
_____
_____.

4. Basic rules for good essays: Well-organized structure

4.1 Questions:

1) How many parts can this text be divided into? What is the main idea of each part?

2) Can you try to rearrange the order of each paragraph and see if the restructuring change the original purpose of the author at all?

4.2 Analysis:

This essay is well-organized, with a clear structure that allows the authors exposition and argumentation flow with ease.

Part one (Paragraph 1): the lead-in

Paragraph 1 is the lead-in or the opener of the whole composition, which introduces the general concepts and beliefs that the whole essay is going to be based upon. The tone of the whole text is set in this part as well.

Part two (Paragraph 2—7): the development

Paragraph 2 and 3 introduces the one side of the contrast between the traditional VS. progressive education, i.e. the traditional side, summarizing the main features of such sort of education practice.

In Paragraph 4 and **Paragraph 5**, the author make some comment on such main features of traditional education by indicating that the knowledge is imposed and enforced, and the intellectual gap between teachers and students are too wide to bridge.

In Paragraph 5, the author warns his followers not to go to extremes in applying his progressive educational philosophy by totally rejecting the practical means at schools.

In Paragraph 6 and 7, the author restates the highlights of his philosophy of progressive education and emphasizes the constructive way in which such education should be carried out.

Part three (Paragraph 8 and 9) : the end

Paragraph 8 and 9 end the whole essay by raising some problems and doubts for further discussion. This ending part also prepares for the incoming of the next chapter.

II. Specific Writing Techniques

1. Development of paragraph by reasoning

Please read the following paragraph and learn how it is developed.

I have not made this brief summary for the purpose of criticizing the underlying philosophy. The rise of what is called new education and progressive schools is of itself a product of discontent with traditional education. In effect it is (I criticism of the latter). When the implied criticism is made explicit it reads somewhat as follows: The traditional scheme is, in essence, one of imposition from above and from outside. It imposes adult standards, subject-matter, and methods upon those who are only growing slowly toward maturity. The gap is so great that the required subject matter, the methods of learning and of behaving are foreign to the existing capacities of the young. They are beyond the reach of the experience the young learners already possess. Consequently, they must be imposed; even though good teachers will use devices of art to cover up the imposition so as to relieve it of obviously brutal features.(Paragraph 4)

Analysis: The process of developing this paragraph is a process of reasoning. Sentence 1 is a transitional sentence that links this paragraph with the previous one. Sentence 2 is a development of sentence 1. And from sentence 3 to the end of this paragraph is the main reasoning process to illustrate why knowledge in traditional education must be imposed, with each sentence being deducted from its previous sentence:

The traditional scheme is, in essence, one of imposition from above and from outside.

⇩

It imposes adult standards, subject-matter, and methods upon those who are only growing slowly toward maturity.

⇩

The gap is so great that the required subject matter, the methods of learning and of behaving are foreign to the existing capacities of the young.

⇩

They are beyond the reach of the experience the young learners already possess.

⇩

Consequently, they must be imposed; even though good teachers will use devices of art to cover up the imposition so as to relieve it of obviously brutal features.

2. Imitation:

Try to develop the following topic sentence into a paragraph by reasoning. You may imitate paragraph 4.

English has to be a compulsory course in college. _____
_____
_____
_____
_____
_____.

III. Your Turn to Write

Please write an essay on the topic about why English has to be compulsory in college. You may imitate Dewey's organization of the text by introducing some misunderstanding in the first part, then analyzing and commenting the root of the misunderstanding in the following part and finally providing your own point of view in the third part. Please pay attention to the basic rules of writing good sentences and good paragraphs.

Pearls of Wisdom

1. Education is a progressive discovery of our own ignorance. —Anonymous

2. Data is not information, information is not knowledge, knowledge is not understanding, and understanding is not wisdom. —Anonymous

3. When I walk along with two others, they may serve me as my teachers. I will select their good qualities and follow them, their bad qualities and avoid them. （三人行，必有我师焉：择其善者而从之，其不善者而改之。 —Translated by James Legge

Text B

Warming up

1. What are the advantages and disadvantages of being a teacher?
2. What do you think are the most significant qualities that a teacher needs?
3. The following text is written by Peter Beidler, a published writer and an editor. The winner of several teaching awards, he was named national Professor of the Year in 1983 by the Council for Advancement and Support of Education and the Carnegie Foundation. Does he fit the good teacher in your imagination?

Every teacher probably asks himself time and again: What are the reasons for choosing teaching as a career? Do the rewards teaching outweigh the trying comments? Answering these questions is not a simple task. Let's see what the author says.

Why I Teach

By Peter G. Beidler

1. Why do you teach? My friend asked the question when I told him that I didn't want to be considered for an administrative position. He was puzzled that I did not want what was obviously a "step up" toward what all Americans are taught to want when they grow up: money and power.

2. Certainly I don't teach because teaching is easy for me. Teaching is the most difficult of the various ways I have attempted to earn my living: mechanic, carpenter, and writer. For me, teaching is a red-eye, sweaty-palm, sinking-stomach profession. Red-eye, because I never feel ready to teach no matter how late I stay up preparing. Sweaty-palm, because I'm always nervous before I enter the classroom, sure that I will be found out for the fool that I am. Sinking-stomach, because I leave the classroom an hour later convinced that I was even more boring than usual.

3. Nor do I teach because I think I know answers, or because I have knowledge I feel compelled[1] to share. Sometimes I am amazed that my students actually take notes on what I say in class!

4. Why, then, do I teach?

5. I teach because I like the pace of the academic calendar. June, July, and August offer an opportunity for reflection, research and writing.

6. I teach because teaching is a profession built on change. When the material is the same, I change — and, more important, my students change.

7. I teach because I like the freedom to make my own mistakes, to learn my own lessons, to stimulate[2] myself and my students. As a teacher, I'm my own boss. If I want my freshmen to learn to write by creating their own textbook, who is to say I can't? Such courses may be huge failures, but we can all learn from failures.

8. I teach because I like to ask questions that

A Critical Reader

[1] Why does the author list so many annoyances of being a teacher at the very beginning?

students must struggle to answer. The world is full of right answers to bad questions. While teaching, I sometimes find good questions.

9. I teach because I enjoy finding ways of getting myself and my students out of the ivory tower and into the real world. I once taught a course called "Self-Reliance[3] in a Technological Society." My 15 students read Emerson, Thoreau, and Huxley. They kept diaries. They wrote term papers.

10. But we also set up a corporation, borrowed money, purchased a run-down house and practiced self-reliance by renovating it. At the end of the semester, we would the house, repaid our loan, paid or taxes, and distributed the profits among the group. So teaching gives me pace, and variety, and challenge, and the opportunity to keep on learning.

11. I have left out, however, the most important reasons why I teach.

12. One is Vicky. My first doctoral student, Vicky was an energetic student who labored at her dissertation[4] on a little-known 14th century poet. She wrote articles and sent them off to learned journals. She did it all herself, with an occasional nudge from me. But I was there when she finished her dissertation, learned that her articles were accepted, got a job and won a fellowship to Harvard working on a book developing ideas she'd first had as my student.

13. Another reason is George, who started as an engineering student, then switched to English because he decided he liked people better than things.

14. There is Jeanne, who left college, but was brought back by her classmates because they wanted her to see the end of the self-reliance house project. I was here when she came back. I was there when she told me that she later became interested in the urban poor and went on to become a civil rights lawyer.

15. There is Jacqui, a cleaning woman who knows more by intuition than most of us learn by analysis. Jacqui has decided to finish high school and go to college.

16. These are the real reasons I teach, these people who grow and change in front of me. Being a teacher is being present at the creation, when the clay begins to breathe[5].

2 Why does the author repeat "I teach because…" over and over rather than combing them into one single paragraph?

3 What do Vicky, George, Jeanne and Jacqui symbolize?

17. A "promotion" out of teaching would give me money and power. But I have money. I get paid to do what I enjoy: reading, talking with people, and asking question like, "What is the point of being rich?"

18. And I have power. I have the power to nudge, to fan sparks, to suggest books, to point out a pathway. What other power matters?

19. But teaching offers something besides money and power: it offers love. Not only the love of learning and of books and ideas, but also the love that a teacher feels for that rare student who walks into a teacher's life and begins to breathe. Perhaps love is the wrong word: magic might be better.

20. I teach because, being around people who are beginning to breathe, I occasionally find myself catching my breath with them.

4 What, in summary, is the most important reason why "I teach"?

Notes

1. **compel** /kəm'pɛl/ *v.* to force, drive, or constrain.
2. **stimulate** /'stimjuleit/ *v.* to rouse to activity or heightened action, as by spurring or goading
3. **Self-Reliance** /'selfri'lains/ *Self-Reliance* is an essay written by American Transcendentalist philosopher and essayist, Ralph Waldo Emerson. It contains the most thorough statement of one of Emerson's recurrent themes, the need for each individual to avoid conformity and false consistency, and follow his or her own instincts and ideas. It is the source of one of Emerson's most famous quotations, "A foolish consistency is the hobgoblin of little minds" (often misquoted by omission of the word "foolish").
4. **dissertation** /ˌdisə'teiʃən/ *n.* A lengthy, formal treatise, especially one written by a candidate for the doctoral degree at a university; a thesis.
5. **The clay begins to breathe.** This sentence has a biblical connotation that "dead things begin to have life" The allusion is from Genesis 2:7, "And the LORD God formed man of the dust of the ground, and breathed into his nostrils the breath of life; and man became a living soul." (The KJB Version)

A Critical Reader (II)

1 Who do you think this text is intended for, teachers or students? Why?

2. Which student's story impresses you most? Why?

3. Can you compare the author with one of your favorite teachers? What's the similarity and difference between them?

A Critical Writer

I. Style and word choice

1.1 Peter Beidler is a writer renowned for his simple but effective use of language in almost all his writings. He is capable of conveying genuine feelings and even passionate emotions through plain, direct words and expressions without any fancy, window dressing show-offs. For example:

I teach because I like to ask questions that students must <u>struggle</u> to answer. <u>The world</u> is full of right answers to bad questions. While teaching, I <u>sometimes</u> find good questions. (Paragraph 7)

The underlined words are called "buzzword", which is simple yet powerful enough. Please try to detect the intention of the author's using of these words and feel the strong feelings that are hidden behind.

Please find from the text at least three other expressions of such buzzword, and analyze them.

_____
_____
_____

1.2 Comparative structure

Model: *There is Jacqui, a cleaning woman who knows more by intuition than most of us learn by analysis.*

Imitation:

1) 通常我们在实践中学习到的知识比课堂上多。

_____.

2) 你应该把更多的钱投入到股市中而不是银行里。

_____.

II. Good structure in the level of paragraph and essay

This essay is well-organized, with an Embedding section (Paragraph _____), an effective Development section (Paragraph _____) and a summarizing Conclusion (Paragraph _____). The whole text is mainly developed by (A. time B. space C. cause and effect D. compare and contrast E. examples)

Please explain how each paragraph leads smoothly and logical to the next one.

Paragraph 2 explains one of the wrong guesses for the reason why I choose to teach, by specifying the disadvantages of teaching. Please rewrite it by emphasizing the advantages of choosing other careers. In your rewriting, try to make best use of the original text both in diction and structure:

The original version:

Certainly I don't teach because teaching is easy for me. Teaching is the most difficult of the various ways I have attempted to earn my living: mechanic, carpenter, writer. For me, teaching is a red-eye, sweaty-palm, sinking-stomach profession. Red-eye, because I never feel ready to teach no matter how late I stay up preparing. Sweaty-palm, because I'm always nervous before I enter the classroom, sure that I will be found out for the fool that I am. Sinking-stomach, because I leave the classroom an hour later convinced that I was even more boring than usual.

Rewriting: Teaching is painstaking and demanding. Unlike mechanics, carpenters and writers, _____

_____. Not being a teacher, _____.

_____.

Paragraph 3 shows a typical misunderstanding of a layman of teaching, who believes teachers are proud of the fact that they know answers. But it is actually not the case. Please supply two more misunderstandings of the same sort and refute them one by one, with two more paragraphs.

Nor do I teach because I think I know answers, or because I have knowledge I feel compelled to share. Sometimes I am amazed that my students actually take notes on what I say in class!

Nor do I teach because _____

_____.

Nor do I teach because _____

_____.

III. Your Turn to Write

Have you been so obsessed with something that others just do not quite understand why? Where does the obsession come from and what makes your determination? Please write your own version by imitating the writing techniques of Beidler's essay.

Pearls of Wisdom

1. Plato is dear to me, but dearer still is truth.   —Anonymous

2. The mediocre teacher tells. The good teacher explains. The superior teacher demonstrates. The great teacher inspires.   —Anonymous

3. Teaching is reminding others that they know just as well as you. You are all learners, doers and teachers.   —Anonymous

Text C

Why Chinese Mothers Are Superior (selected)

By Amy Chua

1. A lot of people wonder how Chinese parents raise such stereotypically successful kids. They wonder what these parents do to produce so many math whizzes and music prodigies, what it's like inside the family, and whether they could do it too. Well, I can tell them, because I've done it. Here are some things my daughters, Sophia and Louisa, were never allowed to do:
   - attend a sleepover
   - have a playdate
   - be in a school play
   - complain about not being in a school play
   - watch TV or play computer games
   - choose their own extracurricular activities
   - get any grade less than an A
   - not be the No. 1 student in every subject except gym and drama
   - play any instrument other than the piano or violin
   - not play the piano or violin

2. When it comes to parenting, the Chinese seem to produce children who display academic excellence, musical mastery and professional success—or so the stereotype goes. WSJ's Christina Tsuei speaks to two moms raised by Chinese immigrants who share what it was like growing up and how they hope to raise their children.

3. Despite our squeamishness about cultural stereotypes, there are tons of studies out there showing marked and quantifiable differences between Chinese and Westerners when it comes to parenting. In one study of 50 Western American mothers and 48 Chinese immigrant mothers, almost 70% of the Western mothers said either that "stressing academic success is not good for children" or that "parents need to foster the idea that learning is fun." By contrast, roughly 0% of the Chinese mothers felt the same way. Instead, the vast majority of

A Critical Reader

[1] How do you feel about those taboos?

[2] What features does the data list have?

the Chinese mothers said that they believe their children can be "the best" students, that "academic achievement reflects successful parenting," and that if children did not excel at school then there was "a problem" and parents "were not doing their job." Other studies indicate that compared to Western parents, Chinese parents spend approximately 10 times as long every day drilling academic activities with their children. By contrast, Western kids are more likely to participate in sports teams.

4. What Chinese parents understand is that nothing is fun until you're good at it. To get good at anything you have to work, and children on their own never want to work, which is why it is crucial to override their preferences. This often requires fortitude on the part of the parents because the child will resist; things are always hardest at the beginning, which is where Western parents tend to give up. But if done properly, the Chinese strategy produces a virtuous circle. Tenacious practice, practice, practice is crucial for excellence; rote repetition is underrated in America. Once a child starts to excel at something—whether it's math, piano, pitching or ballet—he or she gets praise, admiration and satisfaction. This builds confidence and makes the once not-fun activity fun. This in turn makes it easier for the parent to get the child to work even more.

5. Chinese parents can get away with things that Western parents can't. Once when I was young—maybe more than once—when I was extremely disrespectful to my mother, my father angrily called me "garbage" in our native Hokkien dialect. It worked really well. I felt terrible and deeply ashamed of what I had done. But it didn't damage my self-esteem or anything like that. I knew exactly how highly he thought of me. I didn't actually think I was worthless or feel like a piece of garbage.

6. As an adult, I once did the same thing to Sophia, calling her garbage in English when she acted extremely disrespectfully toward me. When I mentioned that I had done this at a dinner party, I was immediately ostracized. One guest named Marcy got so upset she broke down in tears and had to leave early. My friend Susan, the host, tried to rehabilitate me with the remaining guests.

7. The fact is that Chinese parents can do things that would seem unimaginable—even legally actionable—to

Westerners. Chinese mothers can say to their daughters, "Hey fatty—lose some weight." By contrast, Western parents have to tiptoe around the issue, talking in terms of "health" and never ever mentioning the f-word, and their kids still end up in therapy for eating disorders and negative self-image. (I also once heard a Western father toast his adult daughter by calling her "beautiful and incredibly competent." She later told me that made her feel like garbage.)

8. Chinese parents can order their kids to get straight As. Western parents can only ask their kids to try their best. Chinese parents can say, "You're lazy. All your classmates are getting ahead of you." By contrast, Western parents have to struggle with their own conflicted feelings about achievement, and try to persuade themselves that they're not disappointed about how their kids turned out.

9. I've thought long and hard about how Chinese parents can get away with what they do. I think there are three big differences between the Chinese and Western parental mind-sets.

10. First, I've noticed that Western parents are extremely anxious about their children's self-esteem. They worry about how their children will feel if they fail at something, and they constantly try to reassure their children about how good they are notwithstanding a mediocre performance on a test or at a recital. In other words, Western parents are concerned about their children's psyches. Chinese parents aren't. They assume strength, not fragility, and as a result they behave very differently.

11. For example, if a child comes home with an A-minus on a test, a Western parent will most likely praise the child. The Chinese mother will gasp in horror and ask what went wrong. If the child comes home with a B on the test, some Western parents will still praise the child. Other Western parents will sit their child down and express disapproval, but they will be careful not to make their child feel inadequate or insecure, and they will not call their child "stupid," "worthless" or "a disgrace." Privately, the Western parents may worry that their child does not test well or have aptitude in the subject or that there is something wrong with the curriculum and possibly the whole school. If the child's grades do not improve, they may eventually schedule a

3 What does this example imply?

4 What's the point of making this contrast?

meeting with the school principal to challenge the way the subject is being taught or to call into question the teacher's credentials.

12. If a Chinese child gets a B—which would never happen—there would first be a screaming, hair-tearing explosion. The devastated Chinese mother would then get dozens, maybe hundreds of practice tests and work through them with her child for as long as it takes to get the grade up to an A.

13. Chinese parents demand perfect grades because they believe that their child can get them. If their child doesn't get them, the Chinese parent assumes it's because the child didn't work hard enough. That's why the solution to substandard performance is always to excoriate, punish and shame the child. The Chinese parent believes that their child will be strong enough to take the shaming and to improve from it. (And when Chinese kids do excel, there is plenty of ego-inflating parental praise lavished in the privacy of the home.)

> [5] Which side do you take, the western parents or the eastern parents?

14. Second, Chinese parents believe that their kids owe them everything. The reason for this is a little unclear, but it's probably a combination of Confucian filial piety and the fact that the parents have sacrificed and done so much for their children. (And it's true that Chinese mothers get in the trenches, putting in long grueling hours personally tutoring, training, interrogating and spying on their kids.) Anyway, the understanding is that Chinese children must spend their lives repaying their parents by obeying them and making them proud.

15. By contrast, I don't think most Westerners have the same view of children being permanently indebted to their parents. My husband, Jed, actually has the opposite view. "Children don't choose their parents," he once said to me. "They don't even choose to be born. It's parents who foist life on their kids, so it's the parents' responsibility to provide for them. Kids don't owe their parents anything. Their duty will be to their own kids." This strikes me as a terrible deal for the Western parent.

> [6] Do you think what Jed says makes sense? Why?

16. Third, Chinese parents believe that they know what is best for their children and therefore override all of their children's own desires and preferences. That's why Chinese daughters can't have boyfriends in high school and why Chinese kids can't go to sleepaway camp. It's also why no Chinese kid would ever dare say to their

mother, "I got a part in the school play! I'm Villager Number Six. I'll have to stay after school for rehearsal every day from 3:00 to 7:00, and I'll also need a ride on weekends." God help any Chinese kid who tried that one.

17. Don't get me wrong: It's not that Chinese parents don't care about their children. Just the opposite. They would give up anything for their children. It's just an entirely different parenting model.

Notes

1. prodigy /ˈprɔdidʒi/ *n.* a person with exceptional talents or powers
2. quantifiable /ˈkwɔntifaiəbl/ *adj.* that can be quantified, or measured by numbers
3. override /ˌəuvəˈraid/ *v.* to prevail over; conquer
4. ostracize /ˈɔstrəˌsaiz/ *v.* to exclude from a group
5. psyche /saik/ *n.* the spirit or soul
6. foist /fɔist/ *v.* to pass off as genuine, valuable, or worthy

A Critical Writer

I. Use of Extreme Language

This excerpt is taken from the book Battle Hymn of the Tiger Mother by Amy Chua. The book, in which Chua describes her efforts to give her children what she describes as a traditional, strict "Chinese" upbringing, is controversial. Many readers believed that Chua was advocating the "superiority" of a particular, very strict, ethnically defined approach to parenting, to which the author's sharp, satirical, pungent language contributes greatly. Please study the following sentences and pay special attention to the underlined parts.

1. …<u>almost</u> 70% of the Western mothers said either that "stressing academic success is not good for children" or that "parents need to foster the idea that learning is fun." By contrast, <u>roughly 0%</u> of the Chinese mothers felt the same way.

2. …when I was <u>extremely disrespectful</u> to my mother, my father angrily <u>called me "garbage"</u> in our native Hokkien dialect. <u>It worked really well.</u>

3. If a Chinese child gets a B—which would <u>never happen</u>—there would first be a <u>screaming, hair-tearing explosion</u>. The <u>devastated</u> Chinese mother would then get <u>dozens</u>, maybe <u>hundreds</u>

<u>of</u> practice tests and work through them with her child for as long as it takes to get the grade <u>up to an A</u>.

Please find out more of such examples by yourselves.

II. Question for Discussion

Discuss in group about the use of extreme language in this text and about the intention of the author in doing this.

III. Your Turn to Write

Please write about anything you are extremely upset about and try to reveal your anger and grab the reader's attention by using the extreme language like Amy Chua.

Pearls of Wisdom

1. The watchful care of the parent is endless.—Anonymous
2. The first half of our lives is ruined by our parents and the second half by our children. —Anonymous
3. Where parents do too much for their children, the children will not do much for themselves. —Anonymous

Corpus-based Exercises (5)

I. Key Word: education

Education is one of the most commonly-used words in writing. In this Text One alone, the word *education* is used in many different ways:

The rise of what is called new *education* and progressive schools is of itself a product of discontent with traditional *education*.

It is to a large extent the cultural product of societies that assumed the future would be much like the past, and yet it is used as *educational food* in a society

o special talent , no training , no college	**education**	. I didn't think much of myself .
res , the report argues , " undergraduate	**education**	is in trouble . Driven by careerism
Driven by careerism and professional	**education**	, the nation's colleges are more su
uture jobs] than in providing a quality	**education**	. " The document singles out sever

ajor field of study and those of general	education	. Many schools permit students to	5
larm being raised about undergraduate	education	. During the past two years , simila	
e most important argument for a broad	education	is that in studying the accumulate	
. On the contrary , I hated compulsory	education	with a passion . I could never quit	
estructuring to grant women equality in	education	, in employment , in government ,	
mbol upon its students . My homemade	education	gave me , with every additional bo	10
, his feet upon flowers . / In my sensory	education	I include my physical awareness o	
gests a demand for remedial emotional	education	. / And it is here the arguments wil	
itutions and one had died . The median	education	level in the experimental group wa	
extremes , a superior way to approach	education	, perhaps striking a better balance	
I haven't cashed in on that multi-brick	education	and taken on some lawyer-lucrativ	15
reminder about the impact of Distance	education	on the lives of our students who ca	
ready discovered that a convent-school	education	was not at all adequate , and that i	
limitations . First , in classroom-based	education	there is a limitation on the number	
y and time . People are predicting that	education	will be much cheaper in the future	
ncreasing and that makes conventional	education	more expensive than online educa	20
l education more expensive than online	education	. In addition , regular courses (off	
any students who truly need access to	education	. " / Kelley is a successful student	
cators answer students' cries for career	education	, but at the same time let's ensure	
it . In India in the meantime , the entire	education	system has shifted gears to feed th	
to send his daughter to America for her	education	, fearing that same separation . He	25
-class person with a substantial formal	education	, holding a professional or manage	
try have an interest , it is in the decent	education	of the citizens of all parts of the co	

1. Please try to remember the following collocations and expressions of *education* drawn from the above concordance lines.

multi-brick education	quality education	online education
emotional education	professional education	conventional education
homemade education	undergraduate education	classroom-based education
compulsory education	formal education	distance education
general education	access to education	decent education

2. Please translate the following Chinese sentences into English using collocations and expressions of *education* you have learned from Text A and the above concordance lines.

1) 希望工程的主要任务就是为贫困地区的儿童提供上学机会。

2) 九年制义务教育目前已经在我国大部分地区普及。

3) 远程教育技术可以弥补目前课堂教育中的诸多问题。

4) 他之所以能从众多竞争者中脱颖而出获得这个职位，很大程度是因为他良好的个人素质和教育背景。

5) 在传授知识的同时，教师一定不能忽视对学生情感教育。

6) 传统教育更注重知识的积累，而现代教育更强调能力培养。

II. Key Word: knowledge

Knowledge is one of the words that is most frequently used and misused, please study the usage of this word and pay attention to its collocations:

1. Below are concordance lines of *knowledge* taken from CEC, a college English corpus. Try to remember the collocations and expressions of *knowledge* drawn from the following concordance lines. Pay attention, "to learn knowledge" is rarely used in standard English.

meone dedicated to the pursuit of	knowledge	is compared to such a freak . /	
ndergraduates for whom pursuing	knowledge	is the most important thing du	
e teacher is the main source of	knowledge	: He or she lectures , and the st	
oks . Having tasted of the wine of	knowledge	, I could not now alter my cou	
the seeds that later produce	knowledge	and wisdom , then the emotion	5
ld get a base of essential common	knowledge	. Moreover , the major subject	
amassed an incredible amount of	knowledge	in fields far removed from our	
Simonton combined historical	knowledge	about great figures with recent	
n to students that vast store of	knowledge	she has acquired . But because	
s not see himself as an imparter of	knowledge	or a leader of discussion but as	10
made me feel envy of his stock of	knowledge	. Bimbi had always taken char	
ge and , especially , the quest for	knowledge	in high esteem . To contempla	
ne anyone's being more eager for	knowledge	than my Heidi . My little girl .	
solutions based on application of	knowledge	and skills necessary to address	
my children and having gained the	knowledge	that can help them in their futu	15
Web is an excellent way to acquire	knowledge	quickly and easily , visit comp	
arch forces students to look for	knowledge	we don't have . It's a process o	
aff , dedicated to the search for	knowledge	and understanding , who will s	
rson was needed to communicate	knowledge	. He also thinks parents are rec	
ds and studies will become rich in	knowledge	. / — Rich in skill . A person w	20
anscripts that a standard body of	knowledge	has been duly delivered . / Ma	
ds ; they are not the only pool of	knowledge	the students will drink from . I	
al support , as well as distribution	knowledge	. This networking is particular	

e considers it a way to expand his	**knowledge**	. / Jeff's situation raises an int	
om our desks , to grasp and share	**knowledge**	that was beyond the reach of t	25
be otherwise , when the range of	**knowledge**	is so vast that the expert himse	
edulous age , and the burden of	**knowledge**	which we now have to carry is	
so disorganized that I can't retain	**knowledge**	or think at all . The work is stil	
umulated an incredible amount of	**knowledge**	in fields far removed from our	
that enable us to obtain accurate	**knowledge**	about a person (e. g. , disclos	30
With equal passion I have sought	**knowledge**	. I have wished to understand t	
e the older education imposed the	**knowledge**	, methods , and the rules of co	

acquire knowledge	a base of knowledge	common knowledge
become rich in knowledge	application of knowledge	eager for knowledge
gain knowledge	body of knowledge	historical knowledge
impose knowledge	one's stock of knowledge	
obtain knowledge	imparter of knowledge	
produce knowledge	range of knowledge	
retain knowledge	source of knowledge	
search for knowledge	the pursuit of knowledge	
	the quest for knowledge	
	vast store of knowledge	

2. Please translate the following Chinese sentence into English, trying to use the collocations and expressions from the above concordance lines.

1) 政治领导人通常必须具备广博的知识和出众的领导力。

_____

2) 贫困的家境并没有阻止他对知识的追寻。

_____

3) 在场的所有观众都被他惊人的知识储备折服。

_____

4) 知识的应用往往比知识的获取更为重要。

_____

5) 现代信息技术的发达使得教师不再是知识的唯一源头。

_____